*NIHIL OBSTAT*: Reverend Monsignor Richard von Phul Mouton, STD

*IMPRIMATUR*: Most Reverend Michael Jarrell
Bishop of Lafayette
Given at Lafayette, Louisiana, on April 9, 2010

*This book is dedicated to momma and daddy.
We miss you.*

## "How Come?"
## Catholic Apologetics for Cajuns
## Recipes Included!

© Copyright Ed Comeaux 2010
All Rights Reserved

ISBN 1451530072
EAN-13  9781451530070.

Published in the United States of America

All proceeds for the sale of this work benefit the Knights of Columbus, Council 7557, Broussard, La.

Questions or comments to the author are welcome. Please submit comments to edjco@hotmail.com

About the cover: Photograph of Sacred Heart of Jesus Catholic Church, Broussard, La. Photo by the author. Copyright ©Ed Comeaux, 2010. All rights reserved.

**1 Peter 3:15-16:** *"Always be ready to give an explanation to anyone who asks you for a reason for your hope, but do it with gentleness and reverence, keeping your conscience clear, so that, when you are maligned, those who defame your good conduct in Christ may themselves be put to shame."*


*"Preach the Gospel at all times. When necessary, use words."*
**St. Francis of Assisi**

## "How Come?" Catholic Apologetics for Cajuns (Recipes Included!)

**Table of Contents**

Acknowledgements..................................................6

Introduction............................................................7

**Chapter I: The Bible**..................................................13

**Chapter II: The Church**...........................................30

**Chapter III: The Sacraments**......................................59

**Chapter IV Salvation**............................................80

**Chapter V The Blessed Virgin**......................................88

**Chapter VI Christians?**............................................112

**Chapter VII Papal Infallibility**...................................116

**Chapter VIII Idol Worship**......................................123

**Chapter IX Purgatory**...........................................133

**Chapter X Lagniappe**............................................139

**Chapter XI Put the kids to bed, we need to talk**...............175

**Chapter XII Questions for Protestants**........................188

**Chapter XIII Catlick Fax**........................................206

**Chapter XIV Recipes**............................................224

## Acknowledgements

There are a few people who helped me with this book, and they really did make it possible because there is no way that I'm smart enough to have done this on my own.

First and foremost, thanks to Linda Robicheaux, our dear friend and a wonderful schoolteacher who proofed and re-proofed this book since I first began to write it. Linda taught me the correct use of proper pronouns, and even gave me six "smiley faces" on her first proof! In case you didn't know, you only use "it's" when you mean "it is".
Linda, yours is Proverbs 18:24.

There were others who graciously agreed to proof this manuscript and give me words of encouragement, rebuke or both. They are my friends Mary Romero, and Mary Charpentier.
Yours is Proverbs 11:14.

I also have to thank two of my former English teachers who said that I should write something someday. I never forgot that, but after you see my grammar in this book, you may feel otherwise... Thanks so much to Mrs. Dianne Touchet and Mr. Mickey Jung.
Yours is Job 6:24.

Monsignor Richard Mouton was also a great help in his role as Censor Librorum for the Diocese of Lafayette. Monsignor Mouton was responsible for verifying the doctrinal accuracy of this work, and as such had to set me straight a few times... Monsignor, I am proud to call you my friend.

And a very special thanks to my family who put up with me as I wrote this book:

My darling bride Louise, whose encouragement and support really made this possible. I don't think you know how much those late night apologetics discussions helped me.
Yours is Proverbs 31:29-30.

My son Zack, I am so proud. The father is supposed to be the spiritual role model to the son, but many times you have reversed the role.
Yours is Sirach 30:1-6.

And to my daughter Jennifer, you have the gift of finding humor in anything. You have proven to be a wonderful daughter and an exquisite young lady.
Yours is 1 Peter 3:3-4.

## "How Come?"
## Catholic Apologetics for Cajuns
## (Recipes Included!)

**Introduction**

Growing up in South Louisiana years back may have led you to believe that everyone was Catholic. I figured out at a young age that there were people who went to another church besides Sacred Heart. My first clue was that other building in town with the big pointy steeple. My second clue came from my friend Jimmy.

Jimmy and I were in the back yard one day shooting his new Benjamin pellet rifle when he broke the news. (That thing was about as powerful as a .22 when you really got it cranked up.) We were in the middle of our summer vacation and had made it through another Catholic school year. Sister Rose Corrine had no one's ears to pull, thank you very much, because we were free!

That's when Jimmy dropped the bomb: "We're not Catholic, we're Baptists" he said. "What's that?" I asked. (Jimmy attended Catholic school with me, and came to Mass with us during school. I *had* noticed that he didn't kneel and such with the rest of us, but I always thought he was just being lazy.)
"Well, it's like being Catholic, but we don't stand up, sit down and then stand up and then kneel down like Catholics do all the time. We just sit there and sometimes we say 'AMEN' really loud."

Now that was starting to sound pretty good to me; less work at church, and let's face it, after a while, kneeling hurts.

"What else is different?" I asked.

"We don't do communion all the time like ya'll do, just every once in a while," he answered, "and when we do, we have crackers and grape juice instead of the host and wine."

"Well that's weird" I said.

A profound silence followed.

"Do you think a pellet gun would kill a German?" Jimmy asked. (For some reason, we were always obsessed with World War II and killing Germans.)

I thought for a minute: "I guess it would if you're close enough".

We looked at each other, shrugged, and went back to plinking cans.

All issues had officially been decided. Our *"Summit on the Similarities and Differences Between Catholics and Protestants"* was complete. The Pope could finally issue an encyclical because the matter had been decided in the Council of Broussard, the Most Reverend Ed and Jimmy presiding......all was well in the world.

I guess growing up I was always asking "why". Now and then I would wonder why we as Catholics do something, or believe something and I would ask about it.

"Why can't I eat a ham sandwich on Friday?" I once asked.
"Because Father said so." was the usual answer.
Those things never really set well with me. I wondered: "What does Father Jarrell have against ham sandwiches?" or "Why does God insist that I eat fried shrimp on Fridays?" Doesn't really seem like He would care, does it?

A few years ago, Father Jarrell became our Bishop, so he must have been on to something about the whole ham sandwich thing. Anyway, on I went, being a (sometimes) good Catholic kid, serving as an altar boy, but not really knowing the "whys" of my faith.

Then I hit college age and mostly forgot about Church altogether. There was simply too much to do. Those Sunday sleep-ins are much too valuable to waste on going to Church. Why did they ever schedule Mass on Sundays in the first place? Everyone stays out late on Saturday nights at that age, and 9 out of 10 doctors surveyed said that a good night's sleep is very beneficial to your health. Shouldn't Mass be on Monday morning instead? No one would mind missing work or school to go to Church then.

And that's sort of how it was for a few years, although I did start going back to Church sporadically. Still, I never really knew why we believe what we believe. I just jumped in lock-step and followed the crowd. I was determined to do at least the bare minimum to make it to Heaven.

Several years ago, my wife and I were sitting in on a lecture by a local Baptist minister. The topic of the lesson was supposed to be *"A Comparison of Different Faiths"*, which I thought would be pretty interesting. What it turned out to be instead was *"Catholics are basically working for Satan, and everything they believe in is wrong"*.

The speaker would say "Catholics believe….." and I would think, "No we don't". This went on for a couple of hours, and a whole lot of "No, we don'ts", until the thing finally ended. I left there just a tiny bit "angry". Now I know most preachers are not like this, because I've met a lot of them. Most feel like we are all on the same team, all pulling the same rope. I guess what angered me the most was that I knew this particular preacher was wrong, but I didn't know how to defend myself or my faith.

When we got home, I dusted off my *"Catechism of the Catholic Church"* (which in all honesty reads like stereo instructions), my Bible, and anything else I could find remotely related to all things Catholic. After much research, I made what could only be characterized as a grand and eloquent presentation of the faith to my wife. I showed her in no uncertain terms that what was said at the presentation was nothing more than (a little Christian charity here) "mischaracterizations". Great speakers of the world would have stood in awe had they heard me. My wife, however, said the one thing men hate to hear: "That's nice, dear".

Well, so much for my Gettysburg Address. I started wondering what that preacher had against us Catholics.

I soon realized that there are some people in this world who really don't like us just because we are Catholic. I also came to realize that some of these people try to draw Catholics away from the Church because they honestly think they are "saving" us and have the best of intentions.

As I continued to study these issues, I found that almost every time a person of another faith criticizes Catholics, they will incorrectly state what they think we "believe". One of the greatest quotes I ever heard was from Bishop Fulton Sheen. You may remember him on TV if you were around in the day, or you may have seen him on EWTN in re-runs of his old shows. Anyway, here's what Bishop Sheen said:

"Not a hundred people in the United States hate the Roman Catholic Church, but there are millions who hate what they wrongly believe to be the Catholic Church."

Well, that pretty much summed up what I had found. I became determined to learn to defend my Catholic faith, and that's when I discovered the subject of apologetics. Apologetics doesn't mean you have to apologize for being Catholic (unless for some reason you want to) rather, apologetics is defense of the faith.

That, then, is the purpose of this book: to teach Catholics why they believe what they believe, to teach them how to defend their faith, and possibly to teach people of other faiths what Catholics *really* believe.

**BIG CATHOLIC WORD ALERT!!!** Let's just say it up front: The Catholic Church uses some really big words. I know that may come as a shock to you, but it's true. I mean, honestly, did you ever read The Catechism of the Catholic Church? Just right there in the title; what the heck is a 'Catechism'? Sounds like something you would have to bring Tabby to the Vet for. To make matters worse, just when you're about to catch on, they throw a little Latin at you. Anytime I'm forced to use one of those words, I'll warn you with a **BIG CATHOLIC WORD ALERT!!!** That way you can't accuse me of sneaking one in on you…


Lastly, you may be wondering why I chose to include recipes in a Catholic apologetics book. Well, Cajuns love recipes, and that may be the only way to get you to read it!
It is my sincere hope that you enjoy reading this book as much as I have enjoyed writing it.

In Christ,

**Ed Comeaux**

## Chapter One
## The Bible

**"Where da Bible came from?"**

Boudreaux: *"What you reading, Thib?"*
Thibodeaux: *"Mais, I'm readin' my Bible."*
Boudreaux: *"Did you ever wonder, Thib, where the Bible come from?"*
Thibodeaux: *"I don't know, this one came from Wal-Mart."*

But before Wal-Mart, it must have come from somewhere, right? When I was a kid our family had a Bible. Pop and Maw Maw had one too. I'd be willing to bet the Bible was even around when my great grandparents were alive.

So where did it come from? How did we get it? Other Christians tend to criticize Catholics for their "lack of knowledge" of the Bible, so if we want to defend our faith, we should have a better understanding of where the Bible came from in the first place.

Did you know that not all Bibles are the same? It's true. There are actually a whole bunch of different ones, and it may surprise you to know that there can be major differences in Bibles. Let's look at some of those differences and find out exactly where the Bible came from.

As you know the Bible is in two main parts, the Old Testament and the New Testament. Now the Old

Testament is, well, older, so we'll deal with that one first.

Going way back in time, before Pinhook Road was paved, and even before Jesus Himself was just a baby, we had the Old Testament. Now there wasn't a book you could buy somewhere called the Old Testament. Instead, what they had were a bunch of smaller books that they used for religious study and worship. Some were written down, and some were just passed on by word of mouth in a way.

In the 3rd century B.C., way before Christ was born; a group of seventy Jewish scholars translated the Old Testament from Hebrew into Greek. This is the oldest Greek version of the Old Testament and is called the **BIG CATHOLIC WORD ALERT!!!** <u>Septuagint</u>. That big word comes from a big Latin word that means "70". (Get it? Seventy Jewish scholars?)

Now, just as you will find with the New Testament, there were more "little books" which didn't make it into the "big book" called the Old Testament. Those 70 Jewish scholars decided which books to include and which to omit. I bet God helped them pick out which ones to include, and well, that's what we believe.

This will become important later, so read this carefully: The Septuagint included what we call the **BIG CATHOLIC WORD ALERT!!!** <u>Deuterocanonical</u> books. Deuterocanonical means sort of like "also canon", or "second canon". That canon is not those 10 gauge goose guns like they sell at the 3 R Feed Store in Gueydan, or what they fought the civil war with, but it means sort of like the Table of Contents. In other words, which little books get to be included in the bigger book.

Ok, to review, the Septuagint (Old Testament) included the Deuterocanonical books, and there are seven of those Deuterocanonical books in the Old Testament (at least in the Catholic Old Testament). Those books are Judith, Tobit, Maccabees I and II, Wisdom, Ecclesiasticus (also called Sirach) and Baruch.

**I bought the wrong Bible?**

This is when, if you are Catholic, you may be having an "uh-oh" moment, because if your Old Testament doesn't have those seven books, it's not a Catholic Bible-or at least it's not what we consider the WHOLE Bible. Go check real quick, we'll wait.

Did you know that those seven books are in Catholic Bibles, but not in many Protestant Bibles? Well, we'll cover that soon, because many Protestant Bibles are also missing some other parts, like parts of Daniel and Esther.

It's enough to say that the Septuagint, (with the Deuterocanonical books) or what we as Catholics consider the Old Testament, was around, <u>and used by</u>, Jesus and the Apostles. How do we know that? Well, <u>*the Septuagint is quoted from or referenced over 300 times in the New Testament*</u>. Looks to me like that's the Scripture that Jesus used...

"The first Christians knew and used the Septuagint in Greek. It was the only body of Scripture known to Saint

Paul, for the Gospels did not yet exist as a written text when he was first preaching Christianity. His listeners spoke Greek. The Epistle to the Hebrews was doubtless written in Greek, not Hebrew. When Saint Paul invoked the Bible, he did so by reference to the Septuagint. The Gospel writers used it too. When the author of Saint Matthew's Gospel cites the prophecy of Isaiah in Matthew 1:23, he uses the phrasing of the Septuagint which differs very slightly from that of the text in Hebrew.

Many of the names of the books of the Bible, familiar to us now as if they were proper nouns, are actually Greek words surviving from the Septuagint. Examples include *genesis* ('creation' in Greek) and *exodus* ('going out', the exit from Egypt). The title of Deuteronomy is from the Septuagint translation of Deuteronomy 17:18,... The book of Psalms too has a title from the Septuagint, *psalmos* in Greek meaning 'plucking with fingers', for these were hymns sung to the harp."[1]

So, Jesus and the Apostles as well as the earliest Christians used the Septuagint. That means they also used the Deuterocanonical books, since those seven books were part of the Septuagint.

After the whole Septuagint thing, Jesus was born, lived, was crucified and rose from the dead. We all know something about that part. Some of Jesus' followers wrote books about His life, death and resurrection and those were called Gospels. There was also a book written called "The Acts of the Apostles", or "Acts". Guess what that one is about. No, it's not ax, like when you ax a question, it's what the Apostles *did* and what happened after Jesus died.

---

[1] Christopher De Hamel, *"The Book. A History of the Bible"*, *(2001, Phaidon Press)*

Then we start seeing letters, or rather **BIG CATHOLIC WORD ALERT!!!** <u>Epistles</u>. An epistle is like a really formal letter that the I.R.S. would send you. What you had was different little churches in different towns, and sometimes they would need more instruction about things, or sometimes someone in a certain church would cut up a little and need an attitude adjustment. Since they couldn't send an e-mail to that church, Apostles like Peter and Paul would write a letter to set them straight. Luckily, they hung on to those letters, because we would end up needing them later to put in the Bible.

After the death of Jesus, there were all sorts of books written. Over time, these books were passed on by word of mouth, or hand copied, and we end up with a whole boatload of books.

Then, a couple of important things happened. Remember when I said that Jimmy and I settled a matter of our faiths by holding the Council of Broussard? Well, the Jews decided to do the same thing. In about 90 A.D. (*decades after Christ was crucified*), the Jews were having some problems. One of their big problems was that a lot of Jews were converting to Christianity. Now remember those seven Deuterocanonical books? It turns out that those seven books really tended to make Christianity look good, and they really pointed to Jesus as the Messiah, so the Jews had their own Council in a town called Jamnia. They called it the Council of Jamnia, but you saw that one coming. The purpose of that council was to decide which books would be included in their "Old Testament" so to speak.

"...around A.D. 90-100, after the Temple fell, a rabbinical school was formed by Johanan ben Zakkai. The "Council of Jamnia" is the name given to the decisions made by this pharisaic school. I repeat: the gathering at Jamnia was a *Jewish, not a Christian,* "council" consisting of Pharisees some 40 years after the Resurrection of our Lord. At that time, Jews were being scattered, and the very existence of Jewry per the Pharisees' vision of "Jewry" was being threatened. At this time, too, Christianity was growing and threatening that same Jewish identity, resulting in severe persecution of Christians by Jews. In reaction to these things and to the fact that "Nazarenes" (i.e., "Christians", who at that time were overwhelmingly Hebrew) used the Septuagint to proselytize other Jews, Zakkai convened the Jamnian school with the goals of safeguarding Hillel's Oral Law, deciding the Jewish canon (which had theretofore been, and possibly even afterward remained, an *open canon*!), and preventing the disappearance of Jewry into the Diaspora of the Christian and Roman worlds. So, circling their wagons, **they threw out the Septuagint that they had endorsed for almost 400 years.** Note that at the time of Christ, most Jews spoke Aramaic, Latin (the official language of the area), and/or Greek (the lingua franca at that time), not Hebrew, which was a sacred language used by priests for the Hebrew liturgy. In any case, a *new* Greek translation was created by Aquila -- but one without the ancient Septuagint's language that proved more difficult for the Jews to defend against when being evangelized by the Christians, the point being that any idea that a book "had" to have been written in Hebrew to be "Biblical" wasn't the issue."[2]

It may surprise you to know the reasons why the book of Maccabees in particular was removed from the Jewish "Old Testament". The Council of Jamnia was conducted under the authority of the Roman Emperors. They felt that Maccabees, which spoke about the Maccabean Revolt, might incite rebellion by the Jews.

---

[2] Fisheaters, *"The Canon of Scripture"*, http://www.fisheaters.com/septuagint.html

"So, all those Protestant Bibles are lacking the Book of Maccabees, which speaks clearly of praying for the dead, because a pagan emperor pressured the Pharisees, around 40 years after the Resurrection of Christ, to exclude it."[3]

So you have the Christians with their 46 books and some, but not all (post-Jesus) Jews with 39. And as they say, time passed....

While that time was passing, the Christians (again, they had a whole bunch of New Testament era books) wanted to decide the canon of (or what books went into) the New Testament. You will never guess what they did. That's right, they had themselves a Council.

Actually, they held two Councils. One was in 393 in Hippo and was called; now you're catching on, the Council of Hippo. The other Council was in 397 in Carthage, Mississippi (or some other Carthage) and was called the Council of Carthage. These two councils decided which books would be included in the New Testament. These Councils also had some guidance from God, which we will talk about later.

And time passed.... Then, in the 1500's (about **1200 years after** the canon of the Bible was finalized, and we were all very happy with our Bible), there was this Catholic Monk named Martin Luther. Now Martin Luther wasn't happy about some of the things going on in the Catholic Church (nowadays, we would call him a "problem employee"). In some cases he was right, but instead of working from within to change some things, he decided to just break off and make his

---

[3] Fisheaters, *"The Canon of Scripture"*, http://www.fisheaters.com/septuagint.html

own church, and Lord help me Jesus that's when the problems really started.

Luther, for instance, didn't like the practice of selling indulgences. Neither did the Church as it turns out, but you know there's bad apples in every bunch and some of the clergy were doing it anyway. As the Church was trying to correct the situation, Luther packed up and went out on his own. He did what you call "protested" against the Church. He and his followers who "protested" against the Catholic Church were called "Protestants". That makes sense. And then the whole protesting movement was called the **BIG CATHOLIC WORD ALERT!!!** <u>Protestant Reformation</u>. Personally, I think it was more like a Protestant Deformation, cause that's what it did. Besides indulgences, Luther also disagreed with some other things in the Catholic Church, things like intercessory prayers (saints praying for us) and prayers for the dead, to name a few.

The problem for Luther though, was that Scripture supported these beliefs. Luckily for him, a good chunk of the beliefs he was against were; guess where, the Deuterocanonical books! Now Luther didn't want to fight the fight with Scripture against him, so he sort of "adjusted" the Bible. The first thing he "adjusted" was to remove the seven Deuterocanonical books. Then, he removed parts of Daniel and Esther. Then, he called James "an epistle of straw" (not a good term), and decided to remove Revelations from the Bible.

Now his buddies finally talked him into keeping James and Revelation, but the others remained in the trash. Luther also pushed a belief called **BIG CATHOLIC WORD ALERT!!!** Sola Fide. Actually, that was a Big Catholic and Latin Word Alert which means "faith alone". That means that he believed that we get to Heaven on just faith by itself. In other words, all you have to do is have faith in God (without doing good works) and that's good enough right there, no ifs, ands or buts. Now we are going to talk about Sola Fide later, but for now, let's just understand that the Bible didn't support this belief either. So what did ole Luther do? Well, he added a word to the Bible to help support this belief. Here's the original text of the Bible, which is accurately translated in the Catholic Bible, and then there's Luther's. Look it up in your own Bible if you don't believe me:

The Catholic (and original) version- **Romans 3:28** *For we consider that a person is justified by faith apart from works of the law.*

Luther's version- **Romans 3:28** *For we consider that a person is justified by faith alone apart from works of the law.*

So what's the big deal? So what? It's just one word. The first problem is that it's God's Word, and we shouldn't change it, unless we think we are up to God's level and can correct Him when we see fit. The second problem is that it completely changes the meaning of the passage and allows someone to teach the false doctrine of Sola Fide. Sola Fide believers think that you don't have to do *anything* other than have faith in God and you will get to Heaven. Well, Satan has faith in God. He believes in God because they sort of know each other. Satan knows that God exists even more than humans do. But where did he wind up? It ain't Heaven! So apparently it takes something more than faith (belief) alone. Sola Fide reckons on its face, that you don't have to love your neighbor, in fact *you don't even have to love God!* All you have to do is believe in Him, (have faith) nothing else!

Well that makes about as much sense as an accordion player on a deer hunt. The sad thing is that there are many, many Protestants who swear by that belief to this day. (Oh, and by the way, most Protestant Bibles were at some point later corrected to remove the word "alone", but some folks still insist on using the flawed translations.)

Now what did Martin Luther have to say when the Catholic Church complained that he was adding words to Sacred Scripture? This:

**"You also tell me that the Papists are causing a great fuss because St. Paul's text does not contain the word sola (alone), and that my changing of the words of God is not to be tolerated. If your Papist wishes to make a great fuss about the word "alone" (sola), say this to him: "Dr. Martin Luther will have it so and he says that a papist and an \*\*\* are the same thing." Sic volo, sic iubeo, sit pro ratione voluntas. (I will it, I command it; my will is reason enough) For we are not going to become students and followers of the papists. Rather we will become their judge and master."**

Cocky little fella ain't he? You may have noticed he used the word \*\*\*, and I'm sure you can figure out what that word is. Luther's writings often contained expletives, and make for some "interesting" reading.

Modern fans of Martin Luther would be quite surprised by that fact, and most I have found have not read his works. Strangely enough, this was also not mentioned in the movie "Luther".

So, in the end, you wound up with a Bible that was missing seven Old Testament books, parts of Daniel and Esther, had words added or removed, and had some pretty bad translations. In fact, there were later found to be over 3,000 errors in Luther's translation.

This then, or similar versions of it, became the Protestant Bible. By the way, when Luther first re-translated his Bible, where do you think he got the original documents from to make the translation? From the Catholic Church! Luther, while writing a commentary on the Gospel of John, said this:

"We are obliged to yield many things to the Catholics – (for example), that they possess the Word of God, which we received from them; otherwise, we should have known nothing at all about it."[4]

At least Luther admitted that he got the Bible from us, but many people don't know that, and if they do, they sure as heck ain't about to admit it. So what you have is, from the time of Jesus and the Apostles, and for another 1500 years, is one Catholic Church. Then there is a split when Martin Luther and his followers decide to not dance with the one that brung em. They decide to take the instruction manual and "adjust" it to suit their needs. (Oh, and as a preview to a later chapter, some "Catholics" do that too! We call them Cafeteria

---

[4] Martin Luther, Commentary on John, Chapter 6

Catholics. They follow the line and just take the things they want and leave the rest behind. If you think you're not in that group, can we talk about your feelings on contraception? Don't worry about that yet, we'll get to it).

Then, you have this same group, telling us that the Catholic Church doesn't understand the book that the Catholic Church canonized. Tell the truth now. If you are reading one of those scary books by Stephen King, and you don't get some hidden meaning, do you go ask some guy who read the book to get the right answer; or do you ask Stephen King what he meant when he wrote it? It's the same thing. The Catholic Church determined the canon of the Bible (guided by the Holy Spirit), and the Catholic Church was entrusted by God to teach the Bible with His guidance, so the Catholic Church then gets to tell us what it means. And God helps the Church tell us the right thing as we will talk about later.

So now we know that the Jews removed seven books from the Old Testament, and we know that Martin Luther came along much later and removed them also from their version of the Christian Bible.

The Protestants who do reject the Deuterocanonical books say that they do so because the early Jews rejected them. That, first of all, is not entirely true. The Deuterocanonical books were accepted by Greek speaking Jews and those Jews outside of Jerusalem. It wasn't until **decades after Christ's death** that the Deuterocanonical books were rejected by some, but not all, Jews. Also, the Protestant who rejects the Catholic

Bible is following a Jewish council that also rejected Jesus Christ and the revelation of the New Testament. Interestingly, Protestants never seem to question the Catholic canon of the New Testament books.

Recently, in the mid 1940's, the Dead Sea Scrolls were found. Archaeologists found original Old Testament texts in Hebrew, Greek and Aramaic. Know what else was there? The Deuterocanonical books!

Currently, *many Protestant Bibles now include the Deuterocanonical books* as sort of an "appendix". So if the modern Protestant accepts the Deuterocanonical books, I guess he should now agree that intercessory prayers and prayers for the dead (Catholic beliefs) are in fact Scriptural, since they are obvious in the Deuterocanonical books. Oh, and another thing you may need to know: Protestants call the Deuterocanonical books the *Apocrypha*. Now I don't let them get away with that, because like I said, Deuterocanonical means "also canon", whereas Apocrypha has come to mean more like "not canon". They can call it what they want, but so can I.

Here is what the two Catholic Councils which determined the canon of the Bible had to say:

"Besides the canonical Scriptures, nothing shall be read, in the church under the title of divine writings.'. The canonical books are:---Genesis, Exodus, Leviticus, Numbers, Deuteronomy, Joshua, Judges, Ruth, the four books of Kings, the two books of Paraleipomena (Chronicles), Job, the Psalms of David, the five books of Solomon, the twelve books of the (Minor) Prophets, Isaiah, Jeremiah, Daniel, Ezekiel, Tobias, Judith, Esther, two books of Esdras, two books of the Maccabees. The books of the New Testament are:---the four Gospels, the Acts of the Apostles, thirteen Epistles of S. Paul, one Epistle of S. Paul to the Hebrews, two Epistles of S. Peter, three Epistles of S. John, the Epistle of S. James, the Epistle of S. Jude, the Revelation of S. John. Concerning the confirmation of this canon, the transmarine Church shall be consulted." **Council of Hippo, Canon 36 (A.D. 393).**

"[It has been decided] that nothing except the Canonical Scriptures should be read in the church under the name of the Divine Scriptures. But the Canonical Scriptures are: Genesis, Exodus, Leviticus, Numbers, Deuteronomy, Josue, Judges, Ruth, four books of Kings, Paralipomenon two books, Job, the Psalter of David, five books of Solomon, twelve books of the Prophets, Isaias, Jeremias, Daniel, Ezechiel, Tobias, Judith, Esther, two books of Esdras, two books of the Maccabees. Moreover, of the New Testament: Four books of the Gospels, the Acts of the Apostles one book, thirteen epistles of Paul the Apostle, one of the same to the Hebrews, two of Peter, three of John, one of James, one of Jude, the Apocalypse of John." **Council of Carthage III, Canon 47 (A.D. 397).**

And here's a smackdown of Faustus the Manichean by St. Augustine:

"The authority of our books [Scriptures], which is confirmed by agreement of so many nations, supported by a succession of apostles, bishops, and councils, is against you." *Augustine, Reply to Faustus the Manichean, 13:5 (c. A.D. 400).*

Whenscripturewaswrittenitwasoftenwrittenlikethiswithnospacingnopunctuationandnoparagraphbreaksitalsodidnthavethoselittlenumbersthathelpusfindacertainpassage.

Boy, that's annoying, isn't it? It's really hard to read. So don't you think that if you came along over a thousand years later and tried to translate that from English to Greek that you would have a problem? Well, Luther and other translators did also. What the sentence above said was:

"When Scripture was written, it was often written like this; with no spacing, no punctuation and no paragraph breaks. It also didn't have those little numbers that help us find a certain passage."

The Catholic Church decided which books would be included in the Bible and named it the "Bible". The Church preserved the Bible by hand copying it over and over again for the first 1500 years until the printing press was invented. The Church grounds Her beliefs in the Bible and continues to interpret the Bible for Her people. The Catholic Church has the right to call the Bible Her Book. No one who researches Bible history can deny that.

**Mais yeah, I remember we read that at Church.**

Is it true that Catholics don't know their Bible? Many Catholics probably feel that Protestants know the Bible better than they do. Here are a few facts that would surprise most Protestants, and quite a few Catholics, too:

-The Catholic Mass is composed of about 65% Scripture reading.

-The Catholic Mass contains far more actual Scripture reading than the average Protestant service.

- A faithful Catholic who attends Mass regularly will hear almost the entire Bible in a three year period.

So you see, it's not that we don't know the Bible in most cases, it's just that we don't tend to memorize chapter and verse like many Protestants do. You may not know what is said in John 1:29, but I bet if I asked **any** Catholic to finish the following sentence, they can:

"**Lord God, Lamb of God, you ...**_____."

See! You may know your Bible better than you thought.

Would you like to see the entire Mass with Scripture references? Visit this web page:

www.catecheticsonline.com/apologetics_mass.php

Now when you are defending your faith, you will often find you are defending it against (or answering a question from) a Protestant. Protestants have another belief called **BIG CATHOLIC WORD ALERT!!!** Sola Scriptura (Scripture Alone). That means they only listen to what the Bible has to say about matters of faith, nothing else. As Catholics, we listen to what the Bible has to say, and we listen to what the Catholic Church tells us it means (remember, God teaches the

Bible through the Catholic Church). Protestants don't want to hear anything about what the Catholic Church teaches as a defense, they only want Scripture. The neat thing is that you will NEVER find a Catholic doctrine which is contrary to Scripture, so in the rest of this book, that's just what we'll use-Scripture! We will also use the *Catechism of the Catholic Church* when we need to prove what Catholics *really* believe, and we will use the writings of the Early Church Fathers to show what the very earliest Christians (Catholics) actually believed and practiced.

**Recommended Reading**

*Where We Got the Bible, Our Debt to the Catholic Church* by Henry G. Graham.
Henry Graham is a former Calvinist Minister who converted to Catholicism. Originally written in 1911, this book is still readily available through your local Catholic bookstore.

And, anything at all written by the great Catholic apologist John Martignoni is definitely worth reading. You will see John quoted throughout this book, and he has graciously given me permission to quote him. John has a great apologetics website at:

www.biblechristiansociety.com

John is also writing a Catholic Apologetics book called *Apologetics for the Scripturally Challenged*, and it should be a great one, so look for it soon. If you would like to learn more about apologetics, I would also highly recommend you click on the "Newsletter" link on his webpage.

# Chapter Two
# The Church

**Ok, so where the Church came from?**

Now that we know about the Bible, and we learned where the Bible came from, we can start to figure out where the *Church* came from.

If you read your Bible (and you should), you will see that there is often talk about "the church". Here's what Jesus Himself said:

**Matthew 16:18** *"And so I say to you, you are Peter, and upon this rock I will build my church, and the gates of the netherworld shall not prevail against it.*

So if we believe that Jesus speaks the truth, which I do, I see that He built a church. He also said that the gates of hell would not prevail against it.

**Eph 5:25-28** *"...Christ loved the church and gave himself up for her, in order to make her holy by cleansing her without the washing of water by the word, so as to present the church to himself in splendor without a spot or wrinkle or anything of the kind-yes, so that she may be holy and without blemish.*

That sounds to me like Jesus really, really liked the church. In fact, He loved it. Also, Jesus commanded His church to teach and preach, He promised to give it the Holy Spirit (John 14:16) and to be with it Himself until the end of the world (Mat. 28:20). He established ONE church (Eph. 4:4-5), one faith, one baptism:

**Eph 4:4-5:** *...**one body** and one Spirit, as you were also called to the one hope of your call; **one Lord, one faith, one baptism;..."***

Here we see that Jesus established ONE Church. So, it's pretty obvious to me that Jesus established a church. Now we need to figure out *which* church He founded. John Martignoni probably does it best:

"Now, believing that the Bible is the inerrant Word of God, I see that it teaches that Jesus Christ founded a church...one church. I also see that the gates of Hell will not prevail against this church. This church, as the Bible tells us, is the Body of Christ. Christ is intimately linked and identified with this church. In Acts, we see that Paul was persecuting the church, and then later on we see that Jesus asked Paul, "Why are you persecuting Me?" Jesus identifies Himself with this church. It also tells us that this church is the bride of Christ and that the two have become one. It also tells us that, within this church, <u>there are those who have been given the power of binding and loosing on earth, that which will be bound and loosed in Heaven</u>. It also tells us that within the church there are those of whom Jesus says, "He who hears you, hears Me, and he who rejects you, rejects Me."

This church is shown to be the final arbiter in disputes between Christians. This church also has leaders who can say, "We are of God. Whoever knows God listens to us, and he who is not of God does not listen to us. By this we know the spirit of truth and the spirit of error." Also, we see that this church called a council to settle a doctrinal dispute (Acts 15) and that the leaders of this council spoke on behalf of the Holy Spirit. This church has the Holy Spirit guiding it unto all truth. This church has Jesus with it unto the end of the age. Do you doubt any of this? It is all in Scripture!"

We will need to find a church, established in Apostolic times, which has survived, documented, intact, verifiable, which also satisfies Christ's command to the Apostles that they be '<u>one</u>' and that they preach the gospel throughout the world. Our Apostolic Church needs to be <u>one</u> in doctrine and it needs to be universal (by the way, the word "Catholic" means "universal")- spread all over the world - teaching all the nations. It should also settle doctrinal disputes by way of a council.[5]

That sounds like a textbook definition of the Catholic Church to me!

Don't believe me? Here's a list of various churches, courtesy of John Salza at Scripture Catholic (www.scripturecatholic.com) Tell me if you can see which one of these looks like it was established by Jesus.

| Church | Year Established | Founder | Where Established |
| --- | --- | --- | --- |
| **Catholic** | **33** | **Jesus Christ** | **Jerusalem** |
| Orthodox | 1054 | Schismatic Catholic Bishops | Constantinople |
| Lutheran | 1517 | Martin Luther | Germany |
| Anabaptist | 1521 | Nicholas Storch Thomas Munzer | Germany |
| Anglican | 1534 | Henry VIII | England |
| Mennonites | 1536 | Menno Simons | Switzerland |
| Calvinist | 1555 | John Calvin | Switzerland |
| Presbyterian | 1560 | John Knox | Scotland |
| Congregational | 1582 | Robert Brown | Holland |
| Baptist | 1609 | John Smyth | Amsterdam |
| Dutch Reformed | 1628 | Michaelis Jones | New York |
| Congregationalist | 1648 | Pilgrims and Puritans | Massachusetts |
| Quakers | 1649 | George Fox | England |
| Amish | 1693 | Jacob Amman | France |
| Freemasons | 1717 | Masons from four lodges | London |

---

[5] John Martignoni, http://www.biblechristiansociety.com/

| Church | Year Established | Founder | Where Established |
|---|---|---|---|
| Methodist | 1739 | John & Charles Wesley | England |
| Unitarian | 1774 | T. Lindey | London |
| Methodist Episcopal | 1784 | 60 Preachers | Baltimore, MD |
| Episcopalian | 1789 | Samuel Seabury | American Colonies |
| United Brethren | 1800 | Phillip Otterbein Martin Boehn | Maryland |
| Disciples of Christ | 1827 | Thomas Campbell | Kentucky |
| Seventh Day Adventist | 1844 | Ellen White | Washington, NH |
| Christadelphian | 1844 | John Thomas | Richmond, Va. |
| Salvation Army | 1865 | William Booth | London |
| Holiness | 1867 | Methodist | United States |
| Jehovah's Witness | 1874 | Charles Taze Russell | Pennsylvania |
| Christian Science | 1879 | Mary Baker Eddy | Boston |
| Church of God in Christ | 1895 | Various churches | Arkansas |
| Church of Nazarene | 1850-1900 | Various religious bodies | Pilot Point, Tx. |
| Pentecostal | 1901 | Charles F. Parkham | Topeka, KS |
| Aglipayan | 1902 | Gregorio Aglipay | Philippines |
| Assemblies of God | 1914 | Pentecostalism | Hot Springs, AZ |
| Iglesia ni Christo | 1914 | Felix Manalo | Philippines |
| Four-square Gospel | 1917 | Aimee Semple McPherson | Los Angeles, CA |
| United Church of Christ | 1961 | Reformed and Congregationalist | Philadelphia, PA |
| Calvary Chapel | 1965 | Chuck Smith | Costa Mesa, CA |
| United Methodist | 1968 | Methodist and United Brethren | Dallas, Tx. |
| Born-again | 1970s | Various religious bodies | United States |
| Harvest Christian | 1972 | Greg Laurie | Riverside, CA |
| Saddleback | 1982 | Rick Warren | California |
| Non-denom. | 1990s | Various | United States[6]1 |

---

[6] John Salza,, *What is the history of your church?"*
h,ttp://www.scripturecatholic.com/history.html

Mais, that's a lot of churches! In fact, according to the World Christian Encyclopedia,[7] there are over 30,000 Protestant denominations, all with different beliefs of one sort or another:

The "World Christian Encyclopedia" reportedly states that there are 33,830 Christian denominations in the world. Subtract the Catholic Church and the Eastern churches, and you are left with about 33,800 other churches, those descended from the Protestant Reformation.[8]

If a group within a church disagrees with something, they can go off and start another church down the road until you have all these churches. Remember earlier I told you Jesus founded ONE church, and the "gates of the netherworld shall not prevail against it"? That doesn't sound like ONE church to me. And out of the list above, can you see a church that was founded in apostolic times and still exists today, with ONE teaching? I can, the Catholic Church!

*"Well big whopping deal. So what? We still worship Christ, so who cares if your church is 'older' than mine".*

Now that guy actually does have a point. Other Christian churches usually do have Christ at their center, and they do worship Him. In fact, the Catholic Church teaches that they are our "separated brothers and sisters", and that they too will go to Heaven if they are true to their faith. (It's a little more complicated

---

[7] David D. Barrett, *World Christian Encyclopedia,* (Oxford Press, 2001)
[8] *Karl Keating's e-letter*, May 27, 2003, (Catholic Answers, San Diego, Ca.)

than that, but that's the roux of the whole deal). Another thing you have to keep in mind about other Christians is that they are God's kids too. We don't really have a monopoly on Him; He loves us all, just like your momma and daddy do. And if you have kids, you know you don't like it when they fight; well, neither does God.

The point here is that Jesus established one church, and as you will see later, He gave that church special graces. He also taught us how to do things, and if we are to follow Him, I think we ought to do it His way.

**Mais, because Father said so, that's why.**

I attended Cathedral Carmel High School in Lafayette, and we had this priest, Father Doug Courville (we called him Father C.) who taught us religion. Now, Father C. was a real smart aleck.
I can say that, because we have remained friends to this day, and he was instrumental in my wife's conversion to Catholicism. The reason I mention Father C. is because when he met my wife, he started telling her all of these inaccurate stories about my younger days which I feel were grossly misstated.

Anyway, Father C. told my wife he always remembered me:

*"...with those big paws wrapped around the front of his desk, and he would always say '**Mais Father, how come**...?'"*

Now for the record, I checked, and my "paws" aren't really all that big. In my own defense, I *had* to ask a lot of questions, because growing up, any deep theological question posed to my parents or elders was answered with *"Because Father said so, that's why."* I always wondered what the Scriptural basis was for that. I also wondered why we have to listen to the Church in the first place.

Well, it turns out, there *is* something to that. I found that the Church has a certain *authority*. I also found out that you can find that authority in the Bible. I also found that it's been a while since I gave you a big Catholic word alert, so I should probably do that now. There is a thing in the Church called the **"BIG CATHOLIC WORD ALERT!!!"** Magisterium. The Magisterium is the teaching authority of the Church. Just for fun, here's the Catechism of the Catholic Church's definition of Magisterium:

**MAGISTERIUM:** The living, teaching office of the Church, whose task it is to give as authentic interpretation of the word of God, whether in its written form (Sacred Scripture), or in the form of Tradition. The Magisterium ensures the Church's fidelity to the teaching of the Apostles in matters of faith and morals (85, 890, 2033).

See? I told you, sounds like stereo instructions.
Here's my definition: The Church has the authority to tell you what the Bible means, and it has the authority to tell you what Church tradition means.

Now, read this next passage *very* carefully. This is when Jesus appeared to the Disciples in Jerusalem:

**Luke 24:44-45:** *"He spoke to them, 'These are my words that I spoke to you while I was still with you, that everything written about me in the law of Moses and in the prophets and psalms must be fulfilled.'* ***Then he opened their minds to understand the scriptures.***"

Jesus here is speaking to <u>the leaders of the Church.</u> He didn't open the minds of the people walking by on the street to understand the Scriptures; He opened the minds of the Church leaders.

*"Oh, yeah, right! I've heard about some of the things the Catholic Church has done, and what some of its priests have said and done. And I'm supposed to believe that the Catholic Church and its teachings are as you say 'infallible'?"*

Let's get this one out of the way real quick, ok? Critics of the Church confuse the words "impeccable" and "infallible". Impeccable means perfect. We aren't saying that the Pope, a Cardinal, Bishop or Priest is impeccable, they're not. The Pope has a confessor, and regularly goes to confession. The Pope is a sinner, and so are Priests and Bishops, as is every human being.

What infallibility means is that if the designated bunch of Bishops get together (the College of Bishops) and they are speaking in union with the Bishop of Rome (we call him the Pope), and they are speaking on matters of faith and morals, then they are guided by the Holy Spirit, and can't make a mistake. Now read that carefully. *When they are speaking on matters of faith and morals.* Infallibility doesn't allow them to make really good stock picks or guess the lottery numbers, it only applies when they are officially "teaching" us something, or defining something regarding faith and morals.

Here's an example: My current Pastor is Father Louis Richard. I once heard him say a few years ago that the Saints would win the Super Bowl that year. They didn't. See, that didn't prove that the Catholic Church was wrong. He just happened to be wrong (but we can pray…). Father Louis wasn't the College of Bishops or the Pope, and he wasn't speaking on matters of faith and morals, so my guess is, he got absolutely no help from the Holy Spirit about the Super Bowl.

So where do we get the basis for this notion that the Church has some kind of authority that we are supposed to follow? I thought you'd never ask. Here's what Jesus said:

**Luke 10:16** *"Whoever listens to you listens to me. Whoever rejects you rejects me. And whoever rejects me rejects the one who sent me.*

So who is the "you" that Jesus is speaking to here? The Apostles, *the leaders of the Church*. When a Priest becomes a Priest, the Bishop "lays hands on" him as we see in the Bible. Now follow this, because it will be important later, but Father C. and Father Louis can tell you exactly who laid hands on them when they became Priests. Bishop Jarrell can tell you who laid hands on him. That person can tell you who laid hands on him and so on back through time. In fact, we can trace it back all the way to the Apostles. There is an unbroken line of succession from the Apostles right down to your Priest and Bishop. We call that **BIG CATHOLIC WORD ALERT!!!** Apostolic Succession.

(This is so neat: if you go to www.catholic-hierarchy.org you can click on your Bishop and it will show you who consecrated him. [Try it with Bishop Jarrell]. You can then click on that Bishop and so on. It is not yet completed, but you can go a really long way back. They also maintain a complete listing of all the Popes.)

Well, then, if Jesus established a church, and gave certain powers to its leaders (the Apostles), do you think He intended for those powers or that authority to vanish when the last of those Apostles died? Of course not. He would have started a church which was destined to fail within a hundred or so years. The Catholic Church has not failed. It is still "one".

And let me ask you something else. Protestants argue that the powers given to the Apostles by Jesus, including their teaching authority and the authority to forgive sins died when the Apostles died. Read Acts 1:15-26. This is right after Jesus was crucified and Judas had taken his own life. The Apostles met (led by Peter) and chose who Judas' replacement would be. They chose Matthias. Do you think the authority that Christ gave to the Apostles was also passed on to Matthias, or was he somehow "less" of an Apostle than the others? Now, here's Jesus speaking to Peter:

**Matthew 16:18-19** *"And so I say to you, you are Peter, and upon this rock I will build my church, and the gates* *of the netherworld shall not prevail against it. I will give you the keys to the kingdom of heaven. Whatever you bind on earth shall be bound in heaven; and whatever you loose on earth shall be loosed in heaven."*

Here you have Jesus telling Peter that he was building his church on him (Peter) which we covered. Then, Jesus gives him the keys to the kingdom. If there is a gate in Heaven, and Peter has the keys, I guess he's the gatekeeper, right? That means that Peter can decide who does and doesn't get into Heaven in a sense, right?

If that's not plain enough, read the next sentence in that passage again about binding and loosing. God gave men of His Church the power to bind and loose on earth things that would be bound and loosed in Heaven. Binding and loosing were contractual terms in those days, and Jewish religious leaders could also bind or loose the religious "law" if they determined something was not applicable under the law. In other words, they could act sort of like a judge.

And, just as we talked about Apostolic Succession, the Pope can also be traced, unbroken, right back to Peter who got the keys in the first place.

*"Oh boy. Here we go again. You Catholics with your "Peter was the first Pope nonsense". If Peter was the first Pope, and you can trace the Popes all the way to today, well then who was the SECOND Pope?"*

Pope Linus. Now can we get back to the Bible?
(You will actually hear that question a lot from non-Catholics.)

Now we have Jesus telling the Apostles what to do if someone (a sinner) doesn't listen to them:

**Matthew 18:17** *"If he refuses to listen to them, tell it to the church. If he refuses to listen even to the church, then treat him as you would a Gentile or a tax collector.*

Hmmm...Jesus is telling them to use the church to correct someone. And if he won't even listen to the church, treat him like he works for the I.R.S. At this point, you really have to ask yourself again, which of those 30,000 Protestant churches is Jesus talking about? Or, is it maybe another church?

Let's look at one more example, and then we're done with the teaching authority of the Church. Bible meaning can be hard to figure out sometimes, so how can you find truth? Wouldn't you know it; the Bible tells you how to find truth:

**1 Timothy 3:15** *"But in case I am delayed, I write so that you will know how one ought to conduct himself in the household of God, which is **the church** of the living God, **the pillar and foundation of the truth.**"*

Now that's really something! The *Bible* tells us that we are to look to the *Church* to find truth. Again, which of those 30,000 churches is Scripture referring to here? Most have different beliefs of one sort or another, so how can they be the "pillar and foundation of the truth" if they do not have consistent beliefs?

There are some non-Catholics who realize that history, tradition and Scripture are against them but nonetheless justify their beliefs as such:

*"I agree that Jesus founded a church, and it may well have been the Catholic Church, but later on, that church went wrong, and **true** Christians were born of the Reformation.*

Well, then, you are calling Jesus a liar if you believe that. Remember the Scripture passage quoted above that said "…and the gates of the netherworld shall not prevail against it."? If this theory, sometimes called the "Great Apostasy" is true, that means that the gates of hell have, in fact, prevailed against the church that Jesus established. That also means that Jesus spoke a lie, which He is incapable of doing!

So why is it even important that the Church that Christ established have authority? Well, if a Church has no teaching authority from God, how can we be assured that Church teaching on delicate and important matters is correct? For instance, here's an easy question: "Is abortion wrong?" Well, that seems like an easy enough question, but what about in cases of rape or incest? What about if the pregnancy will result in the death of the mother? Can you see how easily an issue can be muddled without guidance from God through His Church?

Catholics and Protestants have worked closely together on issues such as abortion; but yet, consider this Resolution on Abortion by the Southern Baptist Convention:

## "Resolution On Abortion
June 1971

WHEREAS, Christians in the American society today are faced with difficult decisions about abortion; and

WHEREAS, Some advocate that there be no abortion legislation, thus making the decision a purely private matter between a woman and her doctor; and

WHEREAS, Others advocate no legal abortion, or would permit abortion only if the life of the mother is threatened;

Therefore, be it RESOLVED, that this Convention express the belief that society has a responsibility to affirm through the laws of the state a high view of the sanctity of human life, including fetal life, in order to protect those who cannot protect themselves; and

**Be it further RESOLVED, That we call upon Southern Baptists to work for legislation that will allow the possibility of abortion under such conditions as rape, incest, clear evidence of severe fetal deformity, and carefully ascertained evidence of the likelihood of damage to the emotional, mental, and physical health of the mother.**

This resolution was reaffirmed by the SBC in 1974:

### Resolution On Abortion And Sanctity Of Human Life
June 1974

**WHEREAS, Southern Baptists have historically held a high view of the sanctity of human life**, and

WHEREAS, The messengers to the Southern Baptist Convention meeting in St. Louis in 1971 adopted overwhelmingly a resolution on abortion, and

**WHEREAS, That resolution reflected a middle ground between the extreme of abortion on demand <u>and the opposite extreme of all abortion as murder</u>, and**

WHEREAS, That resolution dealt responsibly from a Christian perspective with complexities of abortion problems in contemporary society;

**Therefore, be it RESOLVED, that we reaffirm the resolution on the subject adopted by the messengers to the St. Louis Southern Baptist Convention meeting in 1971, and**

Be it further RESOLVED, that we continue to seek God's guidance through prayer and study in order to bring about solutions to continuing abortion problems in our society."[9]

So they have a "high view of the sanctity of human life" unless the baby is the product of rape or incest, is severely deformed, or may damage the emotional, mental or physical health of the mother? That doesn't seem to me to be something that Jesus would have agreed with. What exactly did the baby in those circumstances do wrong that she should be killed? Is it a human baby with a human soul if conceived with consent, but not a human baby with a human soul if conceived from a rape or incest?

Here's what the Catholic Church teaches, from the Catechism of the Catholic Church:

**2271** Since the first century the Church has affirmed the moral evil of **every** procured abortion. This teaching has not changed and remains unchangeable. Direct abortion, that is to say, abortion willed either as an end or a means, is gravely contrary to the moral law:

---

[9] Southern Baptist Convention, Resolution on Abortion, http://www.sbc.net/resolutions

> You shall not kill the embryo by abortion and shall not cause the newborn to perish.
>
> God, the Lord of life, has entrusted to men the noble mission of safeguarding life, and men must carry it out in a manner worthy of themselves. Life must be protected with the utmost care from the moment of conception: abortion and infanticide are abominable crimes.

**2272 Formal cooperation in an abortion constitutes a grave offense. The Church attaches the canonical penalty of excommunication to this crime against human life.** "A person who procures a completed abortion incurs excommunication *latae sententiae*," "by the very commission of the offense," and subject to the conditions provided by Canon Law. The Church does not thereby intend to restrict the scope of mercy. Rather, she makes clear the gravity of the crime committed, the irreparable harm done to the innocent who is put to death, as well as to the parents and the whole of society.

**2322** From its conception, the child has the right to life. Direct abortion, that is, abortion willed as an end or as a means, is a "criminal" practice (*GS* 27 § 3), gravely contrary to the moral law. The Church imposes the canonical penalty of excommunication for this crime against human life.

**2274** Since it must be treated from conception as a person, the embryo must be defended in its integrity, cared for, and healed, as far as possible, like any other human being.
*Prenatal diagnosis* is morally licit, "if it respects the life and integrity of the embryo and the human fetus and is directed toward its safe guarding or healing as an individual. . . . It is gravely opposed to the moral law when this is done with the thought of possibly inducing an abortion, depending upon the results: a diagnosis must not be the equivalent of a death sentence."

So what does the Catholic Church teach is morally acceptable if for instance, a pregnant mother has uterine cancer?

"The principle of double effect applies: (1) Your intention is to perform a good—to save the mother's life by removing her cancerous uterus. The evil effect of causing the death of the baby is not desired. It is a very sad and unfortunate result of the good act. (2) The evil effect does not cause the good result. You are removing a diseased organ that is killing the mother, not performing an abortion. The baby will die during or shortly after the operation, but the purpose of the operation is not to kill the child. (3) Two very grave matters must be weighed against each other. Saving one person is better than allowing both to die through inaction, even though it means the death of one."[10]

You see, these issues become too big for us humans to discern on our own. That is why it is necessary to have an infallible interpreter of an infallible Scripture. Jesus left us with one-His Church.

Catholics then gain their beliefs from the Bible <u>and</u> from Church Teaching. Protestants gain their beliefs from the Bible only. Let's talk about that.

**Da book, da whole book, and nuttin but da book.**

*"Catholics follow man-made rules. We (non Catholics) follow the inerrant word of God in Scripture, not the rules made by some group of people. "*

Since Protestants do not recognize the authority of the Church, they all share a belief called Sola Scriptura, which means "scripture alone". In other words, they believe that the Holy Spirit guides each individual person in their private interpretation of Scripture, and

---

[10] Matthew Newsome, Catholic Answers, "*Abortion and Double Effect*", (San Diego: Catholic Answers)

that Scripture alone is the sole authority that they use to determine matters of faith and morals.

Well, there are several problems with Sola Scriptura, the first one is found in Scripture:

**2 Peter 1:20** *"Know this first of all, that there is no prophecy of scripture that is a matter of personal interpretation..."*

The way I read it, Sola Scriptura is not Scriptural according to Scripture.

Another problem with Sola Scriptura is that it doesn't make sense. Remember those 30,000 Protestant denominations we talked about? If the Holy Spirit guides each person to an "infallible" interpretation of the Bible, how come there are 30,000 different interpretations? We all know that the Holy Spirit cannot teach error, so how do you explain that?

Here's one practical example of the problem with Sola Scriptura: All Protestant faiths from the time of the Reformation believed that contraception was an evil act up until 1930. Since then, contraception has become "popular" and accepted among Protestants, and therefore allowed in most denominations. If you are guided by Scripture alone, and we know that Scripture is the inerrant word of God, how can faith and morals change with popular opinion?

Now think about that. If I read the Bible and I'm guided by the Holy Spirit and you read the Bible and you are also guided by the Holy Spirit; and we come to different conclusions; then that has to mean that the Holy Spirit either didn't guide one of us, or wrongly guided one of us. So maybe it is just like Jesus said:

**John 14:16-17:** *And I will ask the Father, and he will give you another Advocate to be with you always, the Spirit of truth, which the world cannot accept, because it neither sees nor knows it. But you know it, because it remains with you, and will be in you."*

Again, the "you" to whom Jesus is speaking are the Apostles, the <u>leaders of the Church</u>. So, Jesus promised that the Holy Spirit would be with the leaders of the Church, not with every individual who reads the Bible.

Now how about this: I, as a Catholic, listen to what the Church has to say, and depend on Her teaching when I question something about Scripture. According to the Protestant belief, they rely *solely* on Scripture. But, do they really? The Protestants I know do in fact rely on help to interpret Scripture. They get guidance from their Minister, their Bible study leader, Sunday school teacher, etc. So isn't it possible that their private interpretation of the Bible is indeed guided by men? Or, did they all come to the doctrine of the Trinity on their own, despite the fact that the word is not used in the Bible?

One thing they can never tell me is where they got the word "Trinity", because it's not in the Bible. They also can't tell me where they got the word "Bible", because it ain't in the Bible either! They do, however, believe in both of those things, but how can they if they believe in the "Bible alone"?

Another thing you should ask yourself, and Protestants, is this: We know that for 300 years after Jesus died, the Church had yet to canonize the Bible. We also know that from the time the canon of the Bible was compiled, and all the way to the 1400's when the printing press was invented, there was pretty much no Bible available to the average Christian. Before the printing press, Catholic Monks hand copied the Bible over and over again. Naturally, Bibles then were very expensive. I recently read that in current dollars, a Bible would have been worth about $25,000, so your average Christian didn't own one. For the most part, you had a huge hand-written Bible in each Church, and it was often chained down due to its value. People could read it if they wanted, but most were illiterate anyway.

Now all of that to get to this question: If we as Christians are to be guided solely by Scripture, and there wasn't any canonized Scripture for the first 300 years of Christianity, did God simply abandon those early Christians? Did he leave them with no guide to follow? Of course not! He left them the Church. The same can be said for those Christians who lived between 300 and 1400 A.D. They too, had no Scripture to "solely" guide them, or if they did have access to a Bible, most couldn't read it. They did then what Catholics do now: listen to the Church that Christ established, and also listen to Scripture.

Here's a verse that everyone should carefully consider. It is the last two sentences of the Gospel of John:

**John 21:25** *"There are also many other things that Jesus did, but if these were to be described individually, I do not think the whole world would contain the books that would be written."*

Scripture here is telling us that Jesus did many things that were not included in the Bible. So if we go by Scripture alone, we will not get the whole picture. That's why Jesus established a *Church* to guide us, and that Church continues to use the tradition passed on since the Apostles to guide Her flock.

### Literal/literalist. Literally!

Something else you should know is that the Catholic Church interprets the Bible differently than most Protestants do.

Catholics interpret the Bible in a "literal" sense, and Protestants typically interpret the Bible in a "literalist" sense. Now what does that mean?

The "literal" meaning of a certain passage of Scripture is the meaning that the author wanted to give you. The "literalist" interpretation of a passage of Scripture means: "That's what it says, so that's what it means."

Here's an example that's often used to explain this issue. If you read something in a book that said it was "raining cats and dogs outside", you would interpret that to mean that it was raining really hard. If instead, a thousand years from now, you interpreted it in a "literalist" sense, you would take it to mean that there were dogs and cats falling from the sky, and we know what kind of mess that would make.

Tim LaHaye, co-author of the immensely popular "Left Behind" series, certainly uses the literalist approach in his personal interpretation of Scripture. Offhandedly anti-Catholic, his series of fictional books is about the end times of the world and the relatively new (200 year old) belief in the "Rapture", or, at least his version of the Rapture. This is where I want you to remember a passage quoted earlier in this chapter:

**2 Peter 1:20** *"Know this first of all, that there is no prophecy of scripture that is a matter of personal interpretation..."*

Now compare that to a statement by LaHaye:

**"This is no time in history to avoid the study of future things, which is what prophecy is. If we avoid teaching Christians the basics about prophecy, they will be "tossed to and fro" by false teachers who come to them with cunningly devised fables and interpretations that will deceive them...Christians need to know more about prophecy, not less, for that is the only way for them to be armed with the truth.**
          -Tim LaHaye

I suppose that means that if we follow the above passage from Scripture instead of LaHaye's interpretation of Scripture, we will "be tossed to and fro by false teachers..." Sounds to me like someone has declared himself to be infallible...

Here's what the Catholic Church teaches about interpretation of Scripture:

**"However, since God speaks in sacred Scripture through men in human fashion, the interpreter of sacred Scripture, in order to see clearly what God wanted to communicate to us, should carefully investigate what meaning the sacred writers really intended, and what God wanted to manifest by means of their words.**
-Second Vatican Council, Dogmatic Constitution on Divine Revelation, *Dei Verbum*

## Where's my church? It was here just a minute ago...

The whole idea of Christ establishing a Church is just a bit too much for Protestants to take, I'm afraid, especially when historically the only Church which can make the claim that it is the one established by Christ is the Catholic Church (unless, of course you rewrite history).

Simply put, the Catholic Church is the only one that can trace itself unbroken back to the Apostles, and was in existence then. It is also the **only** Church that maintains the same teachings and beliefs of the Apostles and the earliest Christians. In addition, it is the only Church that even had a *name* as early as 107 A.D.; and we know the name "Catholic Church" was around well before then. In fact, we know that the Church was called "Catholic" about the time that St. John, the Apostle, died.

"The term "Catholic" was applied to the Church at the beginning of the second century by Ignatius, the third bishop of Antioch. During the reign of Emperor Trajan (98-117) Ignatius was taken to Rome to be executed. The exact year of the journey is uncertain, but most scholars estimate it was around 107 or 110. On the way to his death, Ignatius wrote letters to churches he was passing by or through. In his letter to the church of Smyrna, he wrote:

"Wherever the bishop appears, let the people be there, just as wherever Jesus Christ is, there is the Catholic Church."[Epistle to the Smyrneans 8:2.]. This is the first recorded use of the phrase "Catholic Church," but its usage almost certainly precedes Ignatius's letter. He assumed his readers would be familiar with the term, and he uses it in an off-handed manner, suggesting he was not coining a new term, but picking up one already in use."[11]

There also seems to be some indication that the term "Catholic Church" is found in Scripture:

Acts 9:31 (Greek)
ἡ μεν ουν **εκκλησια καθ᾽ὅλης** της ιουδαιας και γαλιλαιας και σαμαρειας ειχεν ειρηνην οικοδομουμενη και πορευομενη τω φοβω του κυριου, και τη παρακλησει του ἁγιου πνευματος επληθυνοντο.

Acts 9:31 (Transliteration)
aye men oon ***ekklaysiaye kath olays*** tays ioodayeas kaye galilayeas kaye samarayas aycon ayraynayn oikodomoomenaye kaye poryoomenaye tow fobow too kurioo kaye tay paraklaysay too agioo pnyoomatos eplaythunonto

Now I'm not some Greek linguist, but I do know that ekklaysiaye (ecclesia) means "church", and "kath olays" means "universal". It seems to me like ecclesia katholays (church universal) could very well be converted to English to read: "catholic church".

---

[11] James Akin, *"Catholic"*, This Rock Magazine, (San Diego, Catholic Answers),

Acts 9:31 (English)
*So **the Church throughout all** Judea and Galilee and Samaria had peace and was built up; and walking in the fear of the Lord and in the comfort of the Holy Spirit it was multiplied.*

By the way, Protestants, when speaking of the early Church, often conveniently call them "early Christians". They fail to use the correct term. They were "early Catholics". There were **no** Christians other than Catholics at that point in time. To call them "early Christians" is merely a convenient way of not admitting that they were Catholics. It is also a convenient way of not admitting that the Protestant faiths did not exist until at least the 1500's.

Christ's Church *can't* be the Catholic Church, so for Protestants, there must be another explanation:

*"We believe that the holy Christian Church is a reality, although it is not an external, visible organization. Because 'man looketh on the outward appearance, but the Lord looketh on the heart' only the Lord knows 'them that are his.' The members of the holy Christian Church are known only to God; we cannot distinguish between true believers and hypocrites. **The holy Christian Church is therefore invisible** and cannot be identified with anyone church body or the sum total of all church bodies. "*[12]

Oh, ok. Makes sense to me. There's no way that the Church that Christ established could be the Catholic Church, so when Scripture mentions "the church", it must be talking about an *invisible church*... I know that

---

[12] John J. Moran, *"Is the Church Visible, or Invisible?"*, This Rock Magazine, (San Diego, Catholic Answers, 1993)

sounds silly, but let's deal with it anyway, since it is an almost universal Protestant belief.

According to Protestant belief, "the church" mentioned in Scripture is <u>all</u> Christian churches which are connected by an invisible bond. Therefore, there is no tangible, identifiable "church" with any historical authority. Once again, this belief is not compatible with Scripture, historical fact or plain old common sense.

Now if we are to believe that, it means that Christ created a church with no visibility and, of course, no authority. Sort of like Jesus built a church, but didn't really do a good job of it.

If the Church Jesus built had no authority, how do you explain the canon of the Bible? If the Catholic Church had no authority from God, and the Catholic Church determined the canon of the Bible, then the Bible that all Christians use is invalid.

And, if the Catholic Church had no authority, how do you explain Christmas and Easter?

The Catholic Church gave us the Gregorian Calendar (named for Pope St. Gregory) which we use to this day, and also set the dates for Christmas and Easter. If the Catholic Church had no authority, how could it set feast days? Were these things and countless others attributable to the Catholic Church just done by some "invisible" church with no authority?

By the way, did you ever stop and think about the word "Christmas"? Christ/mas. Christ--mas. **Christ's Mass**. Oops, now I suppose anti-Catholics will start calling it X-mas, or maybe "winter holiday".

Now, back to work. Does the Bible say that Christ's church is invisible?

**Matthew 5:14-16:** *"You are the light of the world. A city set on a mountain cannot be hidden. Nor do they light a lamp and then put it under a bushel basket; it is set on a lampstand where it gives light to all in the house. Just so, your light must shine before others, that they may see your good deeds and glorify your heavenly Father."*

**Luke 8:16-17:** *"No one who lights a lamp conceals it with a vessel or sets it under a bed: rather, he places it on a lampstand so that those who enter may see the light. For there is nothing hidden that will not become visible, and nothing secret that will not be known and come to light."*

Once again, Jesus here is speaking to the Apostles, the leaders of the Church. Sounds to me like He means for them to be quite visible.

**Matthew 18:17:** *"If he refuses to listen to them, tell the church..."*

Now how can you "tell it to the church" if you can't find it? It's invisible, remember?

**Matthew 16:18-19** *"And so I say to you, you are Peter, and upon this rock I will build my church..."*

But y'all won't be able to see it, cause it's invisible.

**Matthew 16:18-19** *"...and the gates of the netherworld shall not prevail against it."*

Well of course Satan won't prevail against it; he won't be able to even *find* it.

**1 Timothy 3:15** *"But in case I am delayed, I write so that you will know how one ought to conduct himself in the household of God, which is the church of the living God, the pillar and foundation of the truth."*

So Jesus gave us a Church which is the "pillar and foundation of the truth". We could use this Church to know truth, if only we could find it...

I don't know Mary Beth Kremski, but I do know that she is a convert to Catholicism and is a third-order Carmelite. I also know she writes really well. Here is part of what she wrote:

"Did you know that history shows that the New Testament Church didn't disappear or deconstruct? Its apostolic leadership and teaching was handed on from generation to generation without missing a beat—in the Catholic Church. (That's not really a statement of faith so much as a historical fact, attested to by honest historians of all faiths and of no faith: the Catholic Church is the Church Jesus started.)

And on the subject of doctrine, have you ever compared what the apostles taught their followers as recorded in the early Church history with the teaching of the Catholic

Church? If not, how can you say its teaching has fallen away from the ideal of the early Church?

I don't expect you to take my word for it, but what would you say if I told you that what the early Church taught fits perfectly with the doctrine of the Catholic Church? It was hard for me to believe at first, but any honest investigation will prove it's so. Are you willing to look into it? Isn't it a matter of simple justice and integrity not to make accusations before getting the facts?

History shows that the original, divinely instituted structure of the Church still exists in the Catholic Church. And if your honest investigation reveals, as it surely will, that its teaching has remained consistent with that of the early Church, then the Church Jesus founded still exists and has not become "corrupt." If this is so, how could any Christian prefer to belong to another church? Is it easier to believe the Church has failed than to consider the possibility of becoming Catholic?"[13]

If you still don't believe me, do some research and find me a Christian writer who believed in an "invisible church" before the sixteenth century and the Reformation. Betcha can't.

Now let's talk about the Sacraments. Make a pot of coffee, this will be fun.

---

[13] Mary Beth Kremski, *Missing Books and Invisible Churches,* (San Diego, Catholic Answers)

## Chapter Three
## The Sacraments

The Catholic Church has seven Sacraments: Baptism, Holy Eucharist, Confession, Confirmation, Matrimony, Anointing of the Sick and Holy Orders. Protestants typically have two (ordinances): Baptism and Matrimony. Let's talk about some of the Catholic Sacraments.

EAT JESUS????.........Ok, cook some rice...
*The Real Presence in the Eucharist*

There are some things I believe in and really don't understand. For instance, I don't really understand the Holy Trinity, and maybe you don't either, but I believe in It. Another thing I believe in and don't understand is the Real Presence in the Holy Eucharist. I can look at the Bible and the Early Church Fathers and see it right there, plain as day. I just don't really *understand* it. I don't understand why God wants us to eat His flesh and drink His blood. Things like that, the Church calls a Mystery. Not a whodunit book like Nancy Drew, but something that maybe God has not yet fully revealed to us.

Whatever it is, I can clearly see that Jesus said it was so and wanted us to do it. That's enough for me right there. Now, I also see the *effect* that receiving Communion has on me and other Catholics. Why, for instance, do I feel so *grateful* when I receive Communion? Why do I feel so good? I don't know, but I like it! Maybe it's because God is REALLY in me? Ok, let's talk about the Real Presence.

*"Catholics believe that at the Lord's Supper they are actually <u>eating</u> Jesus. They must be cannibals! They can't seem to understand that Jesus was speaking symbolically when he said 'This is my body'. Jesus just meant that this <u>symbolizes</u> His body."*

Remember when I told you that Protestants interpret the Bible in a literalist sense? Well, you will find that sometimes they don't. When they don't interpret the Bible in a literalist sense, it is usually when they are disagreeing with a Catholic belief. This is one of those times. The Bible <u>literalistic ally</u> tells us that we are to eat Jesus' flesh and drink His blood. In fact, the very earliest Christians were often accused of cannibalism because of their belief in the Real Presence. Let's look at why Catholics believe that Christ is actually present in the Eucharist.

We first get a hint of this in Malachi chapter 1, way back in the Old Testament. The author is speaking about abuses and religious indifference in the Jewish community. He talks first about *"...offering polluted food on my altar!"* (Malachi 1:7). The passage later in verse 11 talks about *"...a pure offering"*. In the footnotes to the New American Bible, it says **"In his first chapter, the writer foresees the time when all nations will offer a pure oblation –a prophecy whose fulfillment the church sees in the Sacrifice of the Mass."** So, it talks about polluted <u>food</u> offerings and a "pure offering" to come.

Polluted food offerings would be like leaving oysters in the sun for a while and then putting them on God's altar as a sacrifice. I wouldn't want to do that....

**Psalms 110:4**: *"The Lord has sworn and will not waver: "Like Melchizedek you are a priest forever"*.

Now by definition a priest offers a sacrifice. What sacrifice did Melchizedek offer? Bread and Wine! (Gen. 14:18, but look it up yourself if you don't believe me.) So, when did Jesus offer bread and wine as a sacrifice? The only time was at the Last Supper.

**Matthew 26:26-28** *"....this is my body.....this is my blood"*.

It doesn't say this "symbolizes", or this "represents" my body. It says this IS my body.

**I Corinthians 11:27**: *"Therefore whoever eats the bread or drinks the cup of the Lord unworthily will have to answer for the body and blood of the Lord."*

Why would someone who eats or drinks unworthily have to answer if this service is only a 'memorial'? Think about that for a minute. Why would God make such a big deal over something that's only symbolic?

In a few different places in the Bible, Jesus says we are to eat His flesh. "Eat my flesh" or variations of it are repeated by Jesus six times. Four of the times, the Greek word used actually means "to chew".

Let's read John 6. Come on, go get your Bible. In verse 41 Jesus says that He is the bread that came down from Heaven. The Jews start murmuring. (Trust me, they are about to murmur a lot more). Then Jesus says in verse 51 *"I am the living bread that came down from heaven; whoever eats this bread will live forever...."* At that point, Scripture tells us that the Jews went from murmuring to downright quarreling. They said *"How can this man give us [His] flesh to eat?"* Jesus said to them *"Amen, amen, I say to you, unless you eat the flesh of the Son of Man and drink his blood, you do not have life in you."* What a strange thing for Jesus to say. Why didn't He just tell them "I mean that in a symbolic way."? He didn't say that because that's not what He meant!

John 6:55 *"For my flesh is true food, and my blood is true drink."*

That's pretty vague. I wonder what Jesus could possibly have meant by that?

Then we read that *"many of his disciples who were listening said, "This saying (teaching) is hard: who can accept it?"*

So, <u>why</u> would the disciples say that this was a hard teaching if they understood He was speaking symbolically? If Jesus was just telling them to get together once in a while and have some bread and wine to remember him by, would that be a "hard teaching"?

Jesus said a bit more, but then comes verse 66: *"As a result of this, many [of] his disciples returned to their former way of life and no longer accompanied him."*

Now that's one of the most telling passages about the Real Presence. In many other times in Scripture, when the disciples did not understand something, Jesus would explain. Note that in this instance, Jesus didn't run after them saying: "Wait, wait, you misunderstood. I meant that *symbolically*, not *literally*." He simply let them go. <u>This is the only place in the Gospel where disciples left Him over a doctrinal issue.</u>

### What dem old people said about dat?

When someone challenges Catholic beliefs, it always helps to go back and look at what the old folks said. The old folks of the Catholic Church, what we call the "Early Church Fathers" were people who were trained by, and personally knew the Apostles or their immediate successors. Well, if those people were doing something, or believed something, doesn't that tell you that maybe that's what the Apostles taught them? Luckily, some of those Early Church Father's wrote a lot and we can see what they had to say.

Here's what they thought about the Real Presence in the Eucharist:

-<u>All</u> early Church authors who wrote about the Eucharist believed in the Real Presence.

-Ignatius (he died about the same time as the Apostle John died) wrote *"They confess not the Eucharist to be the flesh of our Savior Jesus Christ, which suffered for our sins and which the Father, of his goodness, raised up again."*

**-No writers in the first 300 years after Christ wrote anything remotely related to any other beliefs concerning the Lord's Supper.**

-For the first thousand years of Christianity there were no exceptions to this belief of the early Church in the Real Presence. This was the universal teaching of the entire Church.

-There was a heresy called Rationalism which attacked the Real Presence. So, in 1215 the Catholic Church held a council to define what early Christians already believed. No one had ever challenged this belief, so it was never a matter of debate.

*"Oh, yeah, you Catholics and your Councils. What those Councils were, were Catholics inventing more of your man made beliefs. The Catholic Church did not even believe in the Real Presence until 1215!*

Now you have to watch out for that argument, because you will get it a lot. What almost always happened in the Church was that Catholics had a certain set of beliefs, and the faithful went right along with those beliefs. Someone would always come along and challenge a certain belief, and in this instance, say *"Christ is not really present in the Eucharist."* Well, then, the Church would decide to answer it. In this case, that is what pretty much everyone believed ever since Christ was on Earth, but here we are 1200 years later having to defend it. So, they would hold a Council to absolutely define what we already believed. Now then, if you get that argument from someone, you have to make it clear that the belief didn't *start* with that

Council, it always was. The Council merely settled the matter once and for all.

Hey, did you ever stop to think what you would do if Jesus appeared to you? Would you drop to your knees or prostrate yourself? Would you even be able to look at Him?

You may not know this, but recently a miraculous event occurred right here in a small Catholic Church in South Louisiana. During Mass, as the priest was speaking the words of consecration, Jesus physically appeared over the altar. The people attending that mass were actually blessed with a *physical* visit from our Savior. What a wonderful thing to happen to those lucky people! I would have loved to have been there.

I spoke to one person who was there who told me that the people attending Mass were invited to actually come forward and physically touch Jesus! According to the man I spoke to, though, people sort of sauntered up to the front as if it were no big deal, and after actually coming into physical contact with God, just shuffled off back to their seats. One man, after touching Jesus, walked directly out of the Church. My friend supposed that the man had something important to do. He was quite shocked, he said, because of the indifference that people showed while in the presence of Christ!

Now I was pulling your leg a bit there, because Jesus did not appear in a vision, but He *was* present. And guess what? That happens *every* time Mass is celebrated. Jesus *physically* shows up and invites you to personally touch Him. Do you run out of Church right away? They ain't giving away free biscuits here, you are actually receiving JESUS! Maybe we need to stop and remember that every now and then.

**Now, a personal note.** This is for some of you Catholics, and especially you Cafeteria Catholics. A recent survey found that *40% of Catholics* do not believe in the Real Presence in the Eucharist. That is sad, and dangerous. If you are one of those, you should probably speak to your priest. This is way too important to take lightly.

**I'm SO sorry...**
*Reconciliation or Confession*

*"Catholics believe that they have to tell their sins to a priest and they believe that a priest,-a MAN, can forgive sins. Only God can forgive sins. All I have to do is ask God's forgiveness and I am forgiven, so why would anyone need to confess to a man?*

Why do Catholics go to Confession (Reconciliation)? First of all, let's clear up one wrong belief that other faiths have about Confession: that the priest has the power, by himself, to forgive sins. As Catholics, we know that this authority comes from God. It is not something the priest does all by himself. It is God who forgives sins, but He does it through the priest. So the priest is acting **BIG CATHOLIC WORD ALERT!!!** *in persona Christi*...in the person of Christ. Jesus Christ acting in and through human beings, to bring about the ministry of reconciliation.

So where do we base our belief that we should confess our sins to a priest? We can start with the Bible:

**John 20:21-23**: *"As the Father has sent me, so I send you." And when he had said this, he breathed on them and said to them, "Receive the holy Spirit. Whose sins you forgive are forgiven them, and whose sins you retain are retained."*

Now look at the first sentence of that passage: "As the Father has sent me, so I send you." Send them where? To do what? To forgive sins just like Jesus did! To recap, Jesus tells them He is sending them, and then he **breathes** on them and tells them they can forgive sins. The only other time in Scripture where God breathes on man is in Gen. 2:7, when God "breathes" divine life into man. When this happens, you know that's a big deal.

**Matthew 9:6-8**: *But that you may know that the Son of Man has authority on earth to forgive sins"-he then said to the paralytic, "Rise, pick up your stretcher, and go home." He rose and went home. When the crowds saw this they were struck with awe and glorified God who had given such authority to <u>men</u>."*

Note here it says "men". Plural. This verse shows that God has given the authority to forgive sins to "men", not just to "a man". Now then, non-Catholics will often agree that the apostles had the authority to forgive sins (which this verse demonstrates), but they say that the authority died when the Apostles died. Well then, they need to prove it, otherwise, the Apostles' successors (the Catholic Clergy) still possess this gift. Where in Scripture is the gift of authority to forgive sins taken away from the Apostles or their successors? I can't find it anywhere, but if you do, be sure to call me.

**2 Corinthians 5:18-20**: *"And all this is from God, who has reconciled us to himself through Christ and <u>given us the ministry of reconciliation</u>, namely, God was reconciling the world to himself in Christ, not counting their trespasses against them and <u>entrusting to us the message of reconciliation</u>. So we are ambassadors for Christ, as if God were appealing through us."*

The ministry of reconciliation was given to the ambassadors of the Church. Those appointed to be ambassadors of God were called and chosen to that ministry by the Lord, i.e. the Apostles and their successors- the ordained ministers of the Church. So, if we go by Protestant belief, Jesus gave us the ministry to forgive sins, but it was taken away even though the Bible never says so.

James 5:15-16 - in verse 15 we see that sins are forgiven by the Priests in the sacrament of the sick. So, this is another example of man's authority to forgive sins on earth. Next, in verse 16, James says "Therefore, confess your sins to one another," in reference to the men talked about in verse 15, the priests of the Church.

**Acts 19:18** – *"And many of those who believed, came confessing and declaring their deeds."*

So, many came to *orally* confess their sins. Oral confession was the practice of the early Church just as it is today.

**Lev. 5:4-6** *"...or if someone, without being aware of it, rashly utters an oath to do good or evil, such as men are accustomed to utter rashly, and then recognizes that he is guilty of such an oath;* **then whoever is guilty in any of these cases shall confess the sin he has incurred***, and as his sin offering for the sin he has committed he shall bring to the Lord a female animal from the flock, a ewe lamb or a she-goat.* **The priest shall then make atonement for his sin.**"

Even under the Old Covenant, God used priests to forgive and atone for the sins of others.

Ok, so we see that Jesus gave the apostles (and their successors) the power to forgive sin. Now how are they to forgive (or retain) these sins unless they know what the sins are? Jesus didn't give them the power to go around reading everyone's mind so they would know their sins. He established an oral confession!

Now I'm not going to do everything for you, but if you want to learn more about the Biblical basis for the Sacrament of Reconciliation, read the following passages:

John 20:21-23
Matthew 9:6-8, 18:18, 3:6
Luke 5:24
Mark 1:5
Acts 19:18

2 Cor. 2:10
James 5:16
Lev. 5:4-6; 19:21-22
1 Timothy 6:12
1 John 1:9
Numbers 5:7
Neh. 9:2-3
Sir. 4:26
Baruch 1:18

"What dem old people said"?

Well, the Early Church Fathers said plenty about confession, so we know the earliest Christians, and the immediate students of the Apostles also shared this belief.

**The Didache-Confess your sins in church**, and do not go up to your prayer with an evil conscience. This is the way of life. . . , On the Lord's Day gather together, break bread, and give thanks, after confessing your transgressions so that your sacrifice may be pure (*Didache* 4:14,14:1 [**A.D.70**]).

**The Letter of Barnabas-**You shall judge righteously. You shall not make a schism, but you shall pacify those that contend by bringing them together. **You shall confess your sins**. You shall not go to prayer with an evil conscience. This is the way of light (*Letter of Barnabas* 19 [**A.D. 74**]).

**Ignatius of Antioch-**For as many as are of God and of Jesus Christ are also with the bishop. And as many as shall, **in the exercise of penance**, return into the unity of the Church, these, too, shall belong to God, that they may live according to Jesus Christ (*Letter to the Philadelphians* 3 [**A.D. 110**]).

**Irenaeus-**[The Gnostic disciples of Marcus] have deluded many women. . . Their consciences have been branded as with a hot iron. **Some of these women make a public confession, but others are ashamed to do this**, and in silence, as if withdrawing from themselves the hope of life of God, they either apostatize entirely or hesitate between two courses (*Against Heresies* 1:22 [**A.D. 189**]).

Check this one out, I really like it:

**Tertullian-**[Regarding confession, some] flee from this work as being an exposure of themselves, or they put it off from day to day. **I presume they are more mindful of modesty than of salvation, like those who contract a disease in the more shameful parts of the body and shun making themselves known to the physicians; and thus they perish along with their own bashfulness** (*Repentance* 10:1 [**A.D. 203**]).

**Hippolytus-**[The bishop conducting the ordination of the new bishop shall pray:] God and Father of our Lord Jesus Christ. . . pour forth now that power which comes from you, from your Royal Spirit, which you gave to your beloved Son, Jesus Christ, and which he bestowed upon his holy apostles. . . and grant this your servant, whom you have chosen for the episcopate, [the power] to feed your holy flock and to serve without blame as your high priest, ministering night and day to propitiate unceasingly before your face and to offer to you the gifts of your holy Church, and by the Spirit of the high priesthood **to have the authority to forgive sins**, in accord with your command (*Apostolic Tradition* 3 [**A.D. 215**]).

**Origen-**[A filial method of forgiveness], albeit hard and laborious [is] **the remission of sins through penance, when the sinner . . . does not shrink from declaring his sin to a priest of the Lord** and from seeking medicine, after the manner of him who say, "I said, to the Lord, I will accuse myself of my iniquity" (*Homilies in Leviticus* 2:4 [**A.D. 248**]).

**Cyprian-**The Apostle [Paul] likewise bears witness and says: "Whoever eats the bread or drinks the cup of the Lord unworthily will be guilty of the body and blood of the Lord "[I Cor. 11:27]. But [the impenitent] spurn and despise all these warnings; before their sins are expiated, **before they have made a confession of their crime, before their conscience has been purged in the ceremony and at the hand of the priest** . . . they do violence to his body and blood, and with their hands and mouth they sin against the Lord more than when they denied him (*The Lapsed* 15:1-3 (**A.D. 251**]).

**John Chrysostom-Priests have received a power which God has given neither to angels nor to archangels**. It was said to them: "Whatsoever you shall bind on earth shall be bound in heaven; and whatsoever you shall loose, shall be loosed."

Temporal rulers have indeed the power of binding: but they can only bind the body. Priests, in contrast, can bind with a bond which pertains to the soul itself and transcends the very heavens. Did [God] not give them all the powers of heaven? "Whose sins you shall forgive," he says, "they are forgiven them; whose sins you shall retain, they are retained." The Father has given all judgment to the Son. And now I see the Son placing all this power in the hands of men [Matt. 10:40; John 20:21-23]. They are raised to this dignity as if they were already gathered up to heaven (*The Priesthood* 3:5 [**A.D. 387**]).

**Here's something interesting:** *Each statement you read above is older than the determination of the canon of the Bible!*

**Keeyaw!**

Did you notice above and in the Bible about public confessions? That's the way it was done for a good while in the early Church. I bet that made adultery almost nonexistent, huh?

Boudreaux: *"I confess to you my brothers and sisters, that Clotile and I..."*

Thibodeaux: *"You did WHAT wit my wife???"*

So you got it good now with the confessional booth. I don't want to hear any more complaining about going to confession.

**Baptism: It ain't swimmin, and it's not a bat.**

*"Catholics baptize babies, and when they do, they just sprinkle (pour) water on the baby's head. No one in the Bible was baptized this way. How can a baby decide to accept Jesus at that age? Everyone in the Bible was baptized by full immersion. The Catholic concept of baptism is not valid, except when they baptize an adult by immersion".*

Many, if not most, Protestants believe that the only acceptable form of baptism is by full immersion, and that only an adult may be baptized. This is called a "believer's baptism". This strict belief, as you will see, is neither Biblical nor historical.

<u>**Infant Baptism**</u>

Let's look at the issue first from the Old Covenant/New Covenant perspective. In the Old Covenant, a person entered into the Covenant by circumcision. This was done when a baby was 8 days old. This was an outward sign that the baby was part of the Covenant with God. In the New Covenant, what would have replaced this? How would someone enter into the New Covenant? Baptism! So if under the Old Covenant babies were allowed, wouldn't it make sense that babies were welcomed into the New Covenant also?

**Acts 2:38-***Peter said to them, "Repent, and each of you be baptized in the name of Jesus Christ for the forgiveness of your sins; and you will receive the gift of the Holy Spirit.*

Now read the next line:

**Acts 2:39**-*"For the promise is for you and your children and for all who are far off, as many as the Lord our God will call to Himself."*

Sounds to me like children were included.

## Immersion Baptism

The Bible never says how much water to use for baptism. The word "Baptize" comes from the Greek language. It means to dip, to bathe, to immerse, or to pour.

Let's also look at **Ezek 36:25-27**, *"I will SPRINKLE clean water upon you and you shall be clean from all your uncleannesses, and from all your idols I will cleanse you. A new heart I will give you, and a new spirit I will put within you...and I will put My Spirit within you..."*

Now what do you think the Bible is talking about here? Water, a new spirit, cleansed of your uncleannesses? Baptism, by sprinkling, that's what!

It doesn't say anywhere in the Bible that a person has to be immersed to be "officially" baptized. If you read all four of the accounts of Jesus' baptism side-by-side in the Gospels, you can make a very strong case for when it says Jesus "came up out of the water," that it doesn't mean He came up from **under** the water, but rather that it means He came up out of the river.

"What dem old people said?"

A really good source for many apologetics arguments is a book called "Early Christian Writings," published by Penguin Books. In it is a copy of one of the earliest, if not the earliest, non-scriptural Christian writings, called the "Didache." In the Didache, written anywhere from the latter part of the 1st century to the early part of the 2nd century, it talks about Baptism:

**"The procedure for baptizing is as follows: after repeating all that has been said, immerse in running water 'In the name of the Father, and of the Son, and of the Holy Ghost'. If no running water is available, immerse in ordinary water. This should be cold, if possible; otherwise warm. If neither is practicable, then pour water three times on the head 'In the name of the Father....''**

(Note: You can also read it online by going to www.newadvent.org, and clicking on the "Fathers" tab. This gives the writings of many of the early Church Fathers. The Didache is down towards the bottom under "Miscellaneous".)

By the way, one can always decide to be fully immersed when baptized into the Catholic Church, and we have all seen this done. In other words, immersion is not a practice that is forbidden by the Church, it is just one that is not used as often as pouring, since we really don't want to dunk an infant. In fact, in the revised form of Initiation into the Catholic Church, the R.C.I.A., the recommended form of baptism for those adults who are entering our

Catholic faith is that of FULL IMMERSION. In the newer Catholic churches being built these days, it is highly recommended that a full immersion Baptismal Font be included in that Church design, especially for the Easter ritual of baptism of RCIA candidates.

**"Thibodeaux and Clotile, sittin in a tree....."**
*Matrimony*

If y'all don't mind, I'd rather talk about Matrimony in the section that covers annulments, so let's just skip it for now. I know some of you Piccadilly eating Cafeteria Catholics want a shot at that one, but be patient.

**"Maw Maw feels bad. Call da Priest."**
*Anointing of the Sick*

Old timers remember this one as the "Last Rites". I don't know for sure, but I think the Church changed the name to stop scaring people. Imagine you are laying in bed sick, and Father comes in to give you the "Last Rites". Now that wouldn't be very encouraging, would it?

Where does Anointing of the Sick come from? Once again, here's what the Bible has to say:

**Mark 6:12-13** *"So they went off and preached repentance. They drove out many demons, and they anointed with oil many who were sick and cured them.*

**James 5:14** *"Is anyone among you sick? He should summon the presbyters of the church, and they should* *pray over him and anoint him with oil in the name of the Lord..."*

So there it is in the Bible. Makes you wonder why other Christians don't have this Sacrament. One reason may be, again, that they feel this power was not handed down when the Apostles died, and this great gift died with them. But once again, there is no mention in the Bible of this power ever being revoked.

**"What da old people said about dat?"**

**Origin** *"The penitent Christian does not shrink from declaring his sin to a priest of the Lord **and from seeking medicine** . . . [of] which the apostle James says: 'If then there is anyone sick, let him call the presbyters of the Church, and let them impose hands upon him, **anointing him with oil in the name of the Lord; and the prayer of faith will save the sick man, and if he be in sins, they shall be forgiven him**'"* (*Homilies on Leviticus* 2:4, around A.D. 250).

In the year 350, Bishop Serapion wrote, *"We beseech you, Savior of all men, you that have all virtue and power, Father of our Lord and Savior Jesus Christ, and we pray that you send down from heaven the healing power of the only-begotten [Son] upon this oil, so that for those who are anointed . . . it may be effected for the casting out of every disease and every bodily infirmity . . . for good grace and remission of sins . . . "* (*The Sacramentary of Serapion* 29:1).

Here's something else you should know: The Sacrament of The Anointing of the Sick also forgives sins, just like you went to confession; and a person does not have to be on his/her deathbed to get the Sacrament. You can ask for this Sacrament if, for instance, you are about to undergo surgery for a serious illness, or plan to do something dangerous, like drive on Highway 90. (Actually, I made that one up.)

# Chapter Four
# Salvation

**How you get there from here?**

Salvation is another major area of disagreement between Catholics and Protestants. In other words, what does it actually take to get to Heaven? Well, that's pretty important to me, so let's talk about that.

*"I always try my best to convert Catholics because they are going to Hell. They have not accepted Jesus Christ as their personal Lord and Savior. They have not been saved. They believe that their 'good works' will get them a ticket to Heaven".*

<u>Have you been saved?</u> Catholics never really know how to answer that question it seems. The reason it is a bit difficult to answer is that we have a different idea of salvation. Protestants typically believe that salvation is a "one point in time event". "I'm saved, so that's it." Catholics see salvation as a process, not a onetime event. The belief that salvation occurs in an instant and is permanent is called "Once Saved, Always Saved", or OSAS. In this chapter, we will look at OSAS and another belief related to salvation called "Sola Fide", or that faith alone (without good works) saves us.

**That's it? I'm done?**

Let's look at OSAS first. The idea here is that a person is either "saved", or "not saved".

Here's what a recent conversation looked like when I was discussing this subject with a Protestant:

**Me:** "So, you are saved. So in other words no matter how much you sin from now on, you will make it to Heaven, right?"

**Him:** (Silence for a bit. It's usually something they haven't really thought through.) "Well, a person who continues to sin after being saved was never really saved in the first place."

**Me:** "Well, then how do you know for sure that you are really saved? Maybe you weren't really saved."

**Him:** (Blank stare…)

**Him:** "Well, yes. Once you are saved, you are saved. That's it."

**Me:** "Tell me something. Do you think Mother Teresa made it to Heaven?" (Just so you know, many, though not all Protestants really love and respect Mother Theresa.)

**Him:** "Well, I would guess that she did. She devoted her life to the poor."

**Me:** "What about Timothy McVeigh? Do you think he made it to Heaven?

**Him:** "I would think not. He killed 165 people, 19 of them children."

**Me:** "Well then how do you explain that? Mother Teresa *was baptized as an infant*, first of all, and Timothy McVeigh was 'saved'. He accepted Jesus as his personal Lord and Savior."

81

**Him:** (Displaying symptoms of apoplexy) "I'll get back to you on that."

I'm sure you are beginning to see that OSAS doesn't make a lot of sense, but it is an extremely common view among Protestants. OSAS believers often will use Scripture passages which show salvation as a past-tense event to bolster their argument. An example is Romans 10:9 **"...for, if you confess with your mouth that Jesus is Lord and believe in your heart that God raised him from the dead, you will be saved."**

The problem with that is they ignore passages which show salvation as a present or future-tense event. One such passage is Philippians 2:12 where Paul tells us to **"work out your own salvation with fear and trembling."** Now remember, Paul here is speaking to people who had already been baptized and therefore "saved" by the OSAS definition. More examples of salvation being also a future-tense event can be found in Romans 13:11 **"For our salvation is nearer now than when we first believed;"** as well as 1 Cor. 3:15 and 5:5. To summarize, Catholics believe that salvation is a past, present **and** future tense event.

So an appropriate response would be "I <u>am</u> saved, I <u>am being</u> saved, and I <u>hope to be</u> saved. Or, even this, if they want a Biblical reference:

I **am** saved (Eph 2:5),
**being** saved (1Cor 1:8)
and **hope** I'll be saved (1Cor 3:12-15).
I'm **working out my salvation** in fear (Phil 2:12),
**with hopeful confidence** in Christ (Rom 5:2).

Since the Catholic concept of salvation is more stringent than that of the Protestant, they should be satisfied with our status since we are Baptized, we do accept Christ as our Savior, we confirm our membership in Christ's Church as adults through the Sacrament of Confirmation, and we regularly are forgiven our sins through Reconciliation as some of them do with the one-time "sinner's prayer".

You may also want to ask the Protestant who challenges your salvation to quote chapter and verse in Scripture that we must "accept Jesus Christ as your personal Lord and Savior". Hint: it's not in Scripture, at least not the way they quote it.

I recently saw this exchange between a Catholic and a Protestant on an Apologetics forum:

**Protestant: Have you accepted Jesus Christ as your Personal Lord and Savior?"**

**Catholic: Of course! But why haven't I seen you in mass each Sunday thanking Him and breaking bread with Him as He commanded you to? Have you accepted Him as yours?**

## Fate is all I need?

Next, let's look at Sola Fida, or the idea that faith alone (without good works) is all that is required for salvation. I do know some Protestants who believe, as Catholics do, that good works *are* a requirement for salvation. They, however, are very much in the minority. The two main pillars of Protestantism are Sola Scriptura, which we discussed, and Sola Fide. Those who as I said are in the minority and don't believe in Sola Fide have just toppled one of the two pillars of their own faith.

Ok, here we go. First of all, some Protestants try to mischaracterize Catholic beliefs by saying that the Church teaches that we are saved by *works alone.* This is not correct; the Church teaches that we are saved by faith *and* good works.

Now there are, of course passages in Scripture that tell us that we are saved by faith. The problem for the Sola Fide argument is that nowhere in Scripture does it say that we are saved by faith "alone". In fact, the only place in the Bible where the words "faith" and "alone" appear together is James 2:24, and that verse disproves the doctrine of Sola Fide:

**James 2:24-26** *"See how a person is justified by works and not by faith alone. And in the same way, **was not Rahab the harlot also justified by works** when she welcomed the messengers and sent them out by a different route? For just as a body without a spirit is dead, **so also faith without works is dead.**"*

(Maybe you see now why Martin Luther called the Book of James "an epistle of straw".)

Now of course we have to have faith, but according to the Bible, how else is man saved?

**Matthew 7:24** *"Everyone who listens to these words of mine **and acts on them** will be like a wise man who built his house on rock.*

**Matthew 7:26** *"And everyone who listens to these words of mine **but does not act on them** will be like a fool who built his house on sand."*

So if you do the will of God, you are wise, if you don't, you are a fool. Isn't "acting" the same thing as a "work"?

So how else is man saved? By producing good fruit (John 15:1-6), by keeping the commandments (Matt 19:17), by denying himself and picking up his cross daily (Luke 9:23), by caring for his family (1Tim 5:8), by eating the flesh and drinking the blood of the Son of Man (John 6:51-58), by forgiving the sins of others (Matt 6:14-15), by feeding the hungry and clothing the naked (Matt 25:31-46), and by loving his brother (1 John 2:9-11).

Remember the earlier section about infant baptism? Catholic apologist John Martignoni used infant baptism during a debate to prove that Catholics do not believe that a person is "saved" by works alone:

"I will show, beyond a shadow of a doubt - for any thoughtful and rational person operating without a preconceived animus against the Catholic Church - that Catholics do not believe one is justified by works. As my proof, I hold up the practice of infant baptism...again, a practice which Martin Luther himself believed to be doctrinally correct. An infant can do no works, whatsoever, in order to be justified. Yet, we believe that an infant is indeed justified, by God's grace alone, through baptism. God, acting on His own, in a completely gratuitous manner, pours His saving grace out upon the infant...entering into covenant with the infant, filling the infant with the Holy Spirit, and making the infant a member of the Body of Christ...all without any work done by the infant. Given that belief, how then can Catholics be accused, by any honest man, of believing one is saved by their works? What work did the infant do in order to be justified? Case closed."

Here's a little more scripture for you to consider:

**Romans 2:6**...God will render to every man according to his faith? Nope, according to his deeds.

**James 2:12-13**...God will judge without mercy those who have shown no faith? Nope, those who have shown no mercy.

**Matthew 6:15**...God will judge you based on your faith? Nope, based on whether or not you forgive others.

**Matthew 25:31-46**...how does God separate the sheep from the goats? By their faith? Nope, by what they have **done**.

**Matthew 7:21** How do we get into Heaven, by crying Lord, Lord? By our faith alone? Nope, by whether or not we have **done** the will of God.

**Rev 20:12** *"I saw the dead, the great and the lowly, standing before the throne, and scrolls were opened. Then another scroll was opened, the book of life.* ***The dead were judged according to their deeds****, by what was written in the scrolls."*

I always wanted to ask a Protestant Pastor who believes in Sola Fide whether or not he preaches to his congregation that tithing is not necessary for salvation. Tithing is a work, isn't it?

In defending against Sola Fide, you may want to simply ask these questions: "Do you have to love God in order to be saved? Do you have to love your fellow man to be saved? In other words, can you break the two great commandments of Christ, and still be saved? In 1 Cor 13:13, it says **"Faith, hope, and love abide, these three, but the greatest of these is love."** Why doesn't it say the greatest of these is faith?

# Chapter Five
# The Blessed Virgin

**Mah Momma Mary**

If you've ever been fishing in the Basin in one of those little cuts off of a main channel, you will probably know what I'm talking about here. I was drifting along with the trolling motor one time, getting a few bites here and there, picking up a bream or sac-a-lait every now and then. It was really quiet and peaceful.

I drifted along, more interested in my cork than where I was going, and all of a sudden I had this *"feeling"*. You ever have those? Well, I got this feeling like *"Hey, dummy! You might want to turn around and look at where you're heading!"* When I turned around I was face to face with a football-sized wasp nest. Well, you can pretty much imagine what happened next. I bet it was funny to watch, but it wasn't really funny to live.

I learned that no matter how gently your boat bumps a bush with a big wasp nest in it, the wasps do not appreciate it. It also does not work very well to apologize to the wasps for having bumped their bush. It also does not help to scream loudly while wildly swinging your arms in the air and running around in circles. The only thing that sort of works is to volunteer to give them your boat (besides, if the water is cool enough, it helps with that stinging feeling).

That's pretty much what happens whenever a Protestant and a Catholic are talking and the Blessed Virgin comes up. Some people call it stirring up a hornet's nest; some call it opening up a can of worms. I call it lip kissing a wasp nest.

I have read the accounts of many Protestants who became Catholic. In almost every instance, when they had satisfied themselves on all other doctrinal issues and decided that Catholicism was the way to go, they almost always in the end had to overcome "the obstacle of Mary". This view of Mary as an obstacle however is relatively new. Martin Luther himself had a deep devotion to the Blessed Virgin, as did other reformers. So, let's cover what they say about us, and what we really believe.

### Mais, she's not God, but she's my momma!

*"Catholics worship Mary. They pray to her. The Bible says 'have no false gods before me', yet Catholics worship Mary as a god. Worship is for God alone."*

Yep. Worship *is* for God alone, and the Catholic Church teaches that and believes it. Here's what the Catechism of the Catholic Church says:

**2113** Idolatry not only refers to false pagan worship. It remains a constant temptation to faith. Idolatry consists in divinizing what is not God. **Man commits idolatry whenever he honors and reveres a creature in place of God**, whether this be gods or demons (for example, satanism), power, pleasure, race, ancestors, the state, money, etc. Jesus says, "You cannot serve God and mammon." Many martyrs died for not adoring "the Beast" refusing even to simulate such worship. Idolatry rejects the unique Lordship of God; it is therefore incompatible with communion with God.

*"But wait, we as Catholics DO honor the Blessed Virgin."*

That's right, but we don't honor her *in place of God*. Mary is not God, but she is His mom. Because she is God's mom, we give her due honor.

*"Your true Catholic colors are showing! Did you just call Mary the '**Mother of God**'? How can Mary be the mother of God when God has always been, and will always be? That's just another indication that Catholics think of Mary as a god."*

So what about that? Well, Mary is Jesus' mother, right? And Jesus is God, right? If Mary is Jesus' mother, and if Jesus is God, then Mary is the "Mother of God!" I really don't understand why some people don't get that.

### What dem old people said?

There are many quotes of the Early Church Fathers referring to the Blessed Virgin as the "Mother of God". Here are just a few:

**Irenaeus-** "The Virgin Mary, being obedient to his word, received from an angel the glad tidings that she would bear God" (*Against Heresies*, 5:19:1 [A.D. 189]). Irenaeus

**Cyril of Jerusalem-** "The Father bears witness from heaven to his Son. The Holy Spirit bears witness, coming down bodily in the form of a dove. The archangel Gabriel bears witness, bringing the good tidings to Mary. The Virgin Mother of God bears witness" (*Catechetical Lectures* 10:19 [A.D. 350]).

**Ephraim the Syrian**- "Though still a virgin she carried a child in her womb, and the handmaid and work of his wisdom became the Mother of God" (*Songs of Praise* 1:20 [A.D. 351]).

Protestants may be a bit surprised about their own history as it relates to Mary the Mother of God. The three "pillars of the reformation", Luther, Calvin, and Zwingli, all believed that Mary was the mother of God:

**Martin Luther**: "In this work whereby she was made the Mother of God, so many and such good things were given her that no one can grasp them... Not only was Mary the mother of Him who is born [in Bethlehem], but of Him who, before the world, was eternally born of the Father, from a Mother in time and at the same time man and God." (The Works of Luther, English translation by Pelikan, Concordia, St. Louis, Vol. 7, page 572)

**John Calvin**: "It cannot be denied that God in choosing and destining Mary to be the Mother of His Son, granted her the highest honor...Elizabeth calls Mary Mother of the Lord, because the unity of the person in the two natures of Christ was such that she could have said that the mortal man engendered in the womb of Mary was at the same time the eternal God." (Calvini Opera, Corpus reformatorum, Braunschweig-Berlin, 1863-1900, Vol. 45, page 348 and 335.)

**Ulrich Zwingli**: "It was given to her what belongs to no creature, that in the flesh she should bring forth the Son of God." ( Zwingli Opera, Corpus reformatorum, Berlin, 1905, in Evang. Luc., Op. Comp., Vol. 6, I, page 639.)

The Catholic Church dogmatically defined Mary as the Mother of God at the Council of Ephesus in AD 431. **This was *one thousand and eighty six years* before the founding of the first Protestant church, and *34 years after the canon of the Bible was defined.***

Now, back to "worshiping Mary". As I said, we don't worship the Blessed Virgin, but we do honor her. Remember where the Bible says to "Honor your father and mother"? Since we know that Jesus was a good Jewish boy, would He have followed this commandment and honored his mother? Did the Angel Gabriel honor Mary in his greeting to her? Did God the Father Himself honor Mary when He chose her to be the pure vessel which would carry His only begotten Son into the world?

Now if God the Father honored Mary, and the Angel Gabriel honored Mary, and Jesus honored Mary, is there something wrong with us imitating their behavior? Aren't we supposed to walk in Jesus' footsteps? Well, that's exactly what Catholics do. But, as you will see, there's even more to the Virgin Mary than meets the eye.

**Hail Mary, I'm prayin' wit you.**

*"You Catholics see Mary as some sort of a mediator between you and God. Read 1 Timothy 2:5 which says 'For there is one God. There is also <u>one mediator</u> between God and the human race, Christ Jesus, himself human, who gave himself as ransom for all.'*

*That just proves that Catholics do not follow Scripture, and follow false gods."*

Protestants do not believe in asking Mary or the saints (not the ones in New Orleans either) to pray for them or to help them. So why do Catholics do this? It might be because we don't ignore other passages of Scripture.

For instance, we don't ignore the passage just before the one quoted above:

**1 Timothy 2:1-4:** *"First of all, then,* ***I ask that supplications, prayers, petitions, and thanksgivings be offered for everyone****, for kings and for all in authority that we may lead a quiet and tranquil life in all devotion and dignity."*

Well, then, I guess it is ok to pray for others. So you may want to ask Protestants whether or not they pray for other people. You may also want to ask them if they ever ask someone else to pray for them. Well, isn't that intercessory prayer? Isn't that like someone acting as a mediator between them and God?

You see, we as Catholics don't believe that the people in Heaven, including Mary and the Saints are "dead". They are in fact, alive in Christ since death has no power to separate us from Christ (Rom. 8:3-8). Those in heaven love us more intensely than they ever could have loved us while on earth. They pray for us constantly (Rev. 5:8), and their prayers are powerful (James 5:16-18). Doesn't it make sense, then, to ask

Mary and the Saints to pray for us just as we would ask a friend or relative to pray for us?

Since we know that God the Father and Jesus both honored Mary, and now we know that Mary, along with the Saints, are praying for us; doesn't it seem like maybe the Virgin Mary's prayers would be sort of like "extra special" to her son? To help explain this a little better, read in your Bible about what happened at The Wedding at Cana.

**John 2:1-5:** *"On the third day there was a wedding in Cana in Galilee, and the mother of Jesus was there. Jesus and his disciples were also invited to the wedding. When the wine ran short, the mother of Jesus said to him, 'They have no wine.' [And] Jesus said to her, 'Woman, how does your concern affect me? My hour has not yet come.' His mother said to the servers, 'Do whatever he tells you."*

What happens here is that some people have a problem and Mary takes that problem to Jesus. Jesus then tells her *"Woman"* (the use of the term woman was not disrespectful as it would be to us today, so don't use that on your wife), *"how does your concern affect me? My hour has not yet come."* So, Mary takes these people's problem to Jesus. Jesus tells her that His time has not yet come. But, what does Mary then do? She tells the servants the same thing she tells us: ***"Do whatever he tells you."*** That's pretty important right there, and that's one of the things the Catholic Church teaches that Mary does for us; she reminds us to do God's will!

Well then what happens? Jesus just got through telling Mary that His time had not yet come, and what does Jesus do? He changes the water into wine! Sort of like Mary changed His mind, or rather, that she *interceded* on behalf of the wedding party and Jesus did what she asked! Something else important here: <u>that was Jesus' first public miracle</u>.

*"You can say what you want. You Catholics pray to Mary. That makes her a god in your eyes. Whether you care to admit it or not, when you pray to someone, you make them a god."*

There's another "mischaracterization". Catholics don't pray TO Mary, we pray THROUGH Mary. We ask the Virgin Mary to take our prayers to God. We don't believe that the Blessed Virgin has the power, on her own, to grant our requests. What she does have, is a special power by way of a special relationship with God, to present our prayers to God on our behalf. So if a prayer is placed before God and it comes from Mary or the other saints, it's sort of like a prayer on steroids.

Now go on your own and read Revelations 5:8-11. This is a scene in Heaven where the elders are presenting prayers to the Lamb. Who do you think they are praying for? Would it make sense that the Saints in Heaven are praying for each other? Or, is it maybe that the prayers are for those on Earth? Of course they are. So if the Saints in Heaven are praying for us, why is it wrong to *ask* them (and Mary, who is also a saint) to present our prayers before God?

Oh, and if you are Protestant, did you notice that this passage mentions incense and priests, both Catholic beliefs?

**Brother from another mother**

*"The Bible makes it clear that Jesus has one or two (maybe more) brothers. Where does the 'perpetual virginity' come from? It is obvious that Jesus had siblings."*

This is another very common argument. It does not pass the tests of Scripture, history or common sense. I think the reason Protestants make this argument is that they just sometimes want to disagree with the Catholic Church whenever possible. So why not attack the Perpetual Virginity of Mary while we're at it? Here's the Catholic take on it:

There are about ten instances in the New Testament where "brothers" and "sisters" of the Lord are mentioned (Matt. 12:46; Matt. 13:55; Mark 3:31-34; Mark 6:3; Luke 8:19-20; John 2:12, 7:3, 5, 10; Acts 1:14; 1 Cor. 9:5). Without getting into all the nuances of languages and their translations, suffice it to say that the word "brother" meant many things then, just as it does today. When a Protestant calls his pastor "brother", does that mean that they share the same parents? Of course not. Here are a couple of examples from the Bible:

Lot is called Abraham's "brother" in Genesis 14:14, but Lot was the son of Haran, who was Abraham's brother (Gen. 11:26-28), so, he was actually Abraham's nephew.

Similarly, Jacob is called the "brother" of his uncle Laban in Genesis 29:15.

Kish and Eleazar were the sons of Mahli. Kish had sons of his own, but Eleazar had no sons, only daughters, who married their "brethren," the sons of Kish. These "brethren" were really their cousins (1 Chr. 23:21-22).

**Try this**

Let's try using common sense while reading the Gospel of Luke. Now I submit to you that Mary, betrothed to Joseph (who was much older than her), had taken a vow of lifetime virginity. I think I can prove it, too, if you follow along with me. Here's the Angel Gabriel speaking to Mary:

**Luke 1:31-34:** *"Behold, you will conceive in your womb and bear a son, and you shall name him Jesus. He will be great and will be called Son of the Most High, and the Lord God will give him the throne of David his father, and he will rule over the house of Jacob forever, and of his kingdom there will be no end. But Mary said to the angel,* **'How can this be, since I have no relations with a man?'**"

The Angel Gabriel tells Mary, "Hey, you're gonna have a son, and well, he's gonna be God." Mary doesn't say "What? My kid is gonna be God????? Here I was worried he wouldn't make the little league team." Well, no, she knew she was talking to an Angel of God, and she got that part. Instead, what does Mary ask? *"How can this be, since I have no relations with a man?"* She didn't ask about the God part, she asked about the conception part **because she had no plans to EVER have relations with a man.**

Here's where common sense comes into play, and you can try this as an experiment. Go find a young lady who is engaged to be married and say to her: "You will bear a child". Now what would that young lady say? Probably something like: "Yeah, I hope to.", or maybe "Well, that's the plan." You don't really think she would answer as Mary did now do you? So, maybe we <u>can</u> at least allow for the possibility that Mary intended to be a lifelong virgin.

Part two of your experiment. Now, go find a young nun who has taken a lifelong vow of chastity and tell her the same thing: "You will bear a child." Do you think the nun will answer you pretty much like Mary answered the Angel Gabriel? I bet she would.

Mary is considered the Ark of the New Covenant. Remember, the Ark contained God's Word and was so sacred that you could not touch it (go read 1 Chronicles 13:10; it wasn't pretty). The Ark was a *container*, or rather, the vessel which held the Word of God. What would the "vessel" be that contained the Word of God in the New Covenant? Mary!

Now we know how special the Old Covenant Ark was to God, so do you think the same applies to the New Covenant Ark? Would the new Ark have to be pure to bear the Son of God into the world? Would the new Ark remain pure, or would God allow the new Ark to be defiled by a man?

Would you like to see examples of the Blessed Virgin as the Ark of the New Covenant? Visit this website: www.agapebiblestudy.com/charts/Mary_Charts_Menu.php

The following is from catholic.com:

Some argue that the new ark is not Mary, but the body of Jesus. Even if this were the case, it is worth noting that 1 Chronicles 15:14 records that the persons who bore the ark were to be sanctified. There would be no sense in sanctifying men who carried a box, and not sanctifying the womb who carried God himself! After all, wisdom will not dwell "in a body under debt of sin" (Wis. 1:4 NAB).[14]

One last thing. I say that Mary remained a virgin through her entire lifetime. Christians for 2000 years have said the same thing, even non-Catholics like Martin Luther and John Calvin agreed. It is the modern Protestant who has questioned this doctrine.

### Queen Momma

*"Catholics call Mary 'Queen of Heaven'. Christ is the King of Heaven. To call Mary Queen of Heaven once again elevates her to the position of a god. Just one more man-made Catholic belief."*

---

[14] Catholic Answers, *Immaculate Conception and Assumption*, (Catholic Answers, San Diego, Ca., 2004)

Yep, that's one of the titles we have for the Blessed Virgin. I'll show you why, too! Let's start with the Old Testament. When we look at the Old Testament, we find much support for the Queenship of Mary. At the time of the historical Israel, next to the King's throne was a second throne. We always think of that throne belonging to the King's wife, but in Israel it belonged to the mother of the king. In Aramaic, the word "Gebirah" means Queen Mother. Gebirah was the official title of the Queen Mother, and was a position of authority and honor. Her role was as advisor to the king, and **advocate of the people**. Anyone who had a petition or sought an audience with the King did so through her.

**1 Kings 2:17-21:** *"He said, 'Please ask King Solomon, who will not refuse you, to give me Abishag the Shunamite for my wife.' 'Very well,' replied Bathsheba, (King Solomon's mom) 'I will speak to the king for you.' Then Bathsheba went to King Solomon to speak for Adonijah, and the king stood up to meet her and paid her homage. **Then he sat down upon his throne, and a throne was provided for the king's mother, who sat at his right.**"*

**Jeremiah 13:18**: *"Say to the king and to the **queen mother**, "Come down from your thrones for your **glorious crowns** will fall from your heads." The cities of the Negev will be shut up and there will be no-one to open them. All Judah will be carried into exile, carried completely away."*

There's plenty more, but as we see, there's an abundance of biblical proof that Mary's Queenship is both proper, and scripturally based. Now, you want to really give a Protestant a stroke? Ask them who the woman is in Revelations 12:1-5.

**Rev 12: 1-5**: *"A great and wondrous sign appeared in heaven; a woman clothed with the sun, with the moon under her feet and a **crown** of twelve stars on her head. She was pregnant and cried out in pain as she was about to give birth. Then another sign appeared in heaven; an enormous red dragon with seven heads and ten horns and seven crowns on his heads. His tail swept a third of the stars out of the sky and flung them to the earth. The dragon stood in front of the woman who was about to give birth so that he might devour her child the moment it was born. **She gave birth to a son, a male child, who will rule all the nations with an iron scepter.** And her child was snatched up to God and to his throne."*

So there's a woman in Heaven, wearing a crown (much like a QUEEN would wear). She gave birth to a male child who will rule all nations with an iron scepter. This child was snatched up to God and his throne. I'm having a lot of trouble figuring out who this woman and this child could possibly be.

*"Wrong again, Mr. Catholic. The Woman in this Passage represents the Church. The twelve stars are the twelve Apostles."*

That's one argument they give, but OOPS! If that's true, then that means the Church gave birth to Jesus!

A comment from John Martignoni:

"However Protestant Bible scholars, realizing the implications of recognizing the figure here to be Mary often simply just deny it. For some reason fundamentalist Protestants looking for a female image in Revelation, prefer the scarlet woman of Revelation 17. Revelation 12 makes them squirm, and they strain to find another interpretation."

**Perfect Fit!**

Of all the things that the woman of Revelation 12 can be, Mary seems to be the perfect fit. The woman is probably a symbol of all of the following: Eve, Israel, the Church and Mary. But aren't we allowed to say that the woman giving birth to Jesus is actually Jesus' mother? In that case, the rest of the meaning really "gels". Mary, although the Mother of Jesus; is also part of the Church and the Mother of all Christians. Check this out:

**Revelations 12:17:** *"Then the dragon became angry with the woman and **went off to wage war against the rest of her offspring**, those who keep God's commandments and bear witness to Jesus."*

So, since we are Christians, Mary is our mom, and she is also the Mother of the Church. Think about this: Since Mary was the first one to say "yes" to Jesus, she was also the first Christian!

Did you ever wonder about this? Why, on Sunday morning did Mary not visit Jesus' tomb? She didn't go because she knew He would not be there! Her faith and submission to God's will never wavered, not even for a moment.

**KEEYAW!!! You saw dat? Mary flew!**

The Assumption of the Blessed Virgin is what we Catholics call a dogma. That means that this belief is set in stone and we ain't backing off. Most non-Catholics aren't too happy about that.

*"Your belief of the Assumption states that Mary ascended into Heaven, body and soul. This was reserved only for Christ Jesus."*

No, Mary was "assumed", not "ascended". Assumed means that her Son brought her up; if she had "ascended", like Jesus did, she would have been able to do that of her own power, something we don't believe. Now what about the statement that no one else was ever assumed, body and soul, into Heaven? Ever heard of Elijah (2 Kings 2:11)? I bet Jesus would extend a similar courtesy to His momma!

This is from catholic.com:

There is also what might be called the negative historical proof for Mary's Assumption. It is easy to document that, from the first, Christians gave homage to saints, including many about whom we now know little or nothing. Cities vied for the title of the last resting place of the most famous saints. Rome, for example, houses the tombs of Peter and Paul, Peter's tomb being under the high altar of St. Peter's Basilica in Rome. In the early Christian centuries relics of saints were zealously guarded and highly prized. The bones of those martyred in the Coliseum, for instance, were quickly gathered up and preserved—there are many accounts of this in the biographies of those who gave their lives for the faith.

It is agreed upon that Mary ended her life in Jerusalem, or perhaps in Ephesus. However, neither those cities nor any other claimed her remains, though there are claims about possessing her (temporary) tomb. And why did no city claim the bones of Mary? Apparently because there weren't any bones to claim, and people knew it. Here was Mary, certainly the most privileged of all the saints, certainly the most saintly, but we have no record of her bodily remains being venerated anywhere.[15]

Remember when we talked about the woman in Revelations 12? Did you notice, she's in heaven, and she has a body? She is "clothed in the sun" and wearing a crown. Sounds to me like her body is in Heaven too!

*"Yeah, but where is the Assumption <u>specifically</u> mentioned in the Bible?"*

I'll just let catholic.com answer that one.

"Since the Immaculate Conception and Assumption are not explicit in Scripture, Fundamentalists conclude that the doctrines are false. Here, of course, we get into an entirely separate matter, the question of *sola scriptura*, or the Protestant "Bible only" theory. There is no room in this tract to consider that idea. Let it just be said that if the position of the Catholic Church is true, then the notion of *sola scriptura* is false. There is then no problem with the Church officially defining a doctrine which is not explicitly in Scripture, so long as it is not in contradiction to Scripture.

The Catholic Church was commissioned by Christ to teach all nations and to teach them infallibly—guided, as he promised, by the Holy Spirit until the end of the world (John 14:26, 16:13). The mere fact that the Church teaches that

---

[15] Catholic Answers, *Immaculate Conception and Assumption,* (Catholic Answers, San Diego, Ca., 2004)

something is definitely true is a guarantee that it is true (cf. Matt. 28:18-20, Luke 10:16, 1 Tim. 3:15)."[16]

Now even though Scripture doesn't *explicitly* mention the Assumption, there are very early Christian writings that do, and the Assumption of the Blessed Virgin has been passed on via Apostolic tradition since the very early Church. This is from an apocryphal book called *The Account of St. John the Theologian of the Falling Asleep of the Holy Mother of God* which was written in about 400 A.D.:

16. Then the Saviour said: Let it be according to your opinion. And He ordered the archangel Michael to bring the soul of St. Mary. And, behold, the archangel Michael rolled back the stone from the door of the tomb; and the Lord said: Arise, my beloved and my nearest *relation;* you who hast not put on corruption by intercourse with man, suffer not destruction of the body in the sepulchre. And immediately Mary rose from the tomb, and blessed the Lord, and falling forward at the feet of the Lord, adored Him, saying: I cannot render sufficient thanks to You, O Lord, for Your boundless benefits which You have deigned to bestow upon me Your handmaiden. May Your name, O Redeemer of the world, God of Israel, be blessed for ever.

17. And kissing her, the Lord went back, and delivered her soul to the angels, that they should carry it into paradise. And He said to the apostles: Come up to me. And when they had come up He kissed them, and said: Peace be to you! as I have always been with you, so will I be even to the end of the world. And immediately, when the Lord had said this, He was lifted up on a cloud, and taken back into heaven, and the angels along with Him, carrying the blessed Mary into the paradise of God. And the apostles being taken up in the clouds, returned each into the place allotted for his

---

[16] Catholic Answers, *Immaculate Conception and Assumption,* (Catholic Answers, San Diego, Ca., 2004)

preaching, telling the great things of God, and praising our Lord Jesus Christ, who lives and reigns with the Father and the Holy Spirit, in perfect unity, and in one substance of Godhead, forever and ever. Amen.

I suppose if you do not believe in Sacred Tradition passed on to us by the Apostles and their successors, it may be difficult to understand the Assumption of the Blessed Virgin. That Tradition has nonetheless been passed on to us, as these writings of the Early Church Fathers show:

"If the Holy Virgin had died and was buried, her falling asleep would have been surrounded with honour, death would have found her pure, and her crown would have been a virginal one...Had she been martyred according to what is written: 'Thine own soul a sword shall pierce', then she would shine gloriously among the martyrs, and her holy body would have been declared blessed; for by her, did light come to the world." **Epiphanius, Panarion, 78:23 (A.D. 377).**

"[T]he Apostles took up her body on a bier and placed it in a tomb; and they guarded it, expecting the Lord to come. And behold, again the Lord stood by them; and the holy body having been received, He commanded that it be taken in a cloud into paradise: where now, rejoined to the soul, [Mary] rejoices with the Lord's chosen ones..." **Gregory of Tours, Eight Books of Miracles, 1:4 (inter A.D. 575-593).**

"As the most glorious Mother of Christ, our Savior and God and the giver of life and immortality, has been endowed with life by him, she has received an **eternal incorruptibility of the body** together with him who has raised her up from the tomb and has taken her up to himself in a way known only to him." **Modestus of Jerusalem, Encomium in dormitionnem Sanctissimae Dominae nostrae Deiparae semperque Virginis Mariae (PG 86-II,3306),(ante A.D. 634).**

"It was fitting ...that the most holy-body of Mary, God-bearing body, receptacle of God, divinised, **incorruptible**, illuminated by divine grace and full glory ...should be entrusted to the earth for a little while and raised up to heaven in glory, with her soul pleasing to God." ***Theoteknos of Livias, Homily on the Assumption (ante A.D. 650).***

"You are she who, as it is written, appears in beauty, and your virginal body is all holy, all chaste, entirely the dwelling place of God, so that it is henceforth **completely exempt from dissolution into dust**. Though still human, it is changed into the heavenly life of incorruptibility, truly living and glorious, undamaged and sharing in perfect life." ***Germanus of Constantinople, Sermon I (PG 98,346), (ante A.D. 733).***

"St. Juvenal, Bishop of Jerusalem, at the Council of Chalcedon (451), made known to the Emperor Marcian and Pulcheria, who wished to possess the body of the Mother of God, that Mary died in the presence of all the Apostles, but that her tomb, when opened upon the request of St. Thomas, was found empty; wherefrom the Apostles concluded that the body was taken up to heaven." ***John of Damascene, PG (96:1) (A.D. 747-751).***

"It was fitting that the she, who had kept her virginity intact in childbirth, should keep **her own body free from all corruption even after death**. It was fitting that she, who had carried the Creator as a child at her breast, should dwell in the divine tabernacles. It was fitting that the spouse, whom the Father had taken to himself, should live in the divine mansions. It was fitting that she, who had seen her Son upon the cross and who had thereby received into her heart the sword of sorrow which she had escaped when giving birth to him, should look upon him as he sits with the Father, It was fitting that God's Mother should possess what belongs to her Son, and that she should be honored by every creature as the Mother and as the handmaid of God." ***John of Damascene, Dormition of Mary (PG 96,741), (ante A.D. 749).***

Did you notice in the above passages how Mary's body is incorruptible? That is actually somewhat common among Catholic saints. If you would like to learn more about this subject, I recommend you read "The Incorruptibles" by Joan Carroll Cruz. You may also want to research St. Silvan who died in about 350 A.D. His body is still on display to this day at the Cathedral of St. Blase in Dubrovnik, Croatia.

**Hail Mary, full of grace...**

*"Well, what about the 'Hail Mary'? Catholics pray this prayer to her."*

In case you aren't Catholic, here's the Hail Mary:

Hail Mary, full of grace, the Lord is with thee. Blessed art thou amongst women, and blessed is the fruit of thy womb, Jesus. Holy Mary, Mother of God, pray for us sinners, now, and at the hour of our death. Amen.

When Catholics recite the Hail Mary, we are reciting Scripture.

**Hail Mary, full of grace, the Lord is with thee,** (Luke 1:28)

**Blessed art thou amongst women, and blessed is the fruit of thy womb, Jesus** (Luke 1:42)

The last sentence is not from Scripture, at least not directly, so let's look at it.

**Holy Mary,** (I think we can all assume that she's holy.)

**Mother of God,** (We already covered that one.)

**Pray for us sinners, now and at the hour of our death. Amen.** And here we are just asking her to pray for us, as was also covered.

So, by praying the Hail Mary, we are just repeating Scripture!

Here are a few interesting things about the Blessed Virgin. Scripture speaks of Mary as **"Woman"** in four great citations:

Mary is the woman referenced when God spoke to Satan:

**Genesis 3:15** *"And I will put enmity between you and the **woman**, and between your offspring and hers; he will crush your head, and you will strike his heel."*

Since Jesus is the one who crushes Satan, Mary is the woman who is talked about here.

You may also find this interesting: Until fairly recently, Bible translations said "...*she* will crush your head, and you will strike at *her* heel". The original text basically said something like "...the former will crush your head and you will strike at the former's heel", so it was not readily apparent who does the crushing-although we know it is ultimately "her seed", Jesus. Modern translators have in many cases decided to use he/his rather than she/her. My Douay-Rheims Bible (translated from the Vulgate around 1582-1609) uses "she/her". My New American Bible uses "he/his".

**John 2:1-5:** *"On the third day there was a wedding in Cana in Galilee, and the mother of Jesus was there. Jesus and his disciples were also invited to the wedding. When the wine ran short, the mother of Jesus said to him, 'They have no wine.' [And] Jesus said to her, '**Woman**, how does your concern affect me? My hour has not yet come.' <u>His mother said to the servers, 'Do whatever he tells you.</u>"*

**John 19:26-27:** *"When Jesus saw his mother and the disciple there whom he loved, he said to his mother, '**Woman**, behold, your son.' Then he said to the disciple, <u>'Behold, your mother.' And from that hour the disciple took her into his home.</u>"*

**Revelations 12:17:** *"Then the dragon became angry with the **woman** and went off to wage war against <u>the rest of her offspring</u>, those who keep God's commandments and bear witness to Jesus."*

So, you have four great passages where the term "woman" is used and in those same passages a reference to her "offspring" in one sort or another. These offspring are referred to as:

-offspring,
-servers,
-son,
-offspring, those who keep God's commandments and bear witness to Jesus.

That looks like a bit more than a coincidence to me, and did you ever wonder why we even have John

19:26-27? What is that supposed to mean? Why did Jesus, right before He died, give Mary and the disciple John to each other as mother and son? Do you think Jesus meant anything by that?

Since Mary tells us to "Do whatever He tells you", and since Jesus gave John (the only disciple not martyred) to Mary and Mary to John, and since the "offspring" of Mary are "those who keep God's commandments and bear witness to Jesus", it looks to me like Jesus gave Mary to <u>all of us</u> to be our spiritual mother. Oh, and another thing: Did you ever notice that John is called "the disciple whom Jesus loved"? Does that translate to all of us in any way?

**The last thing I gotta say.**

Here's Elizabeth speaking to Mary:

**Luke 1:45** *"**Blessed are you** who believed that what was spoken to you by the Lord would be fulfilled."*

And from the Canticle of Mary:

**Luke 1:48:** *"For he has looked upon his handmaid's lowliness; behold, **from now on will all ages call me blessed.**"*

My Church calls her "Blessed". Does yours?

## Chapter Six
## Christians?

*"Are y'all Christian?"*

Yes Virginia, you actually do hear that, and quite often. Here's the definition of a Christian from dictionary.com:

**Chris·tian - a person who believes in Jesus Christ; an adherent of Christianity.**

Can I make it any simpler than that? A person who follows Christ is a Christian. So why do we get this ridiculous question so often? First of all, I think it's because some people are just that uninformed. That makes me think about something, though. One of the things that non-Catholic Christians criticize us for is our practice of using a crucifix rather than a cross (we use crosses also). A crucifix is a cross with the figure of Christ crucified on it. A cross is a cross without a figure of Christ. Now, if they can criticize us for using a crucifix, shouldn't that knowledge be just the tiniest hint that we are, in fact, Christians?

There's another reason we get this question, though. The reason in my opinion is because some Protestant faiths seem to spend a good bit of time wondering about this church or that church and whether or not they "are Christians". This may come as a shock to you, but the Southern Baptist Convention feels that *Southern Baptists* may or may not be Christian. It seems there is some disagreement *within their own faith* as to whether or not some Southern Baptists are Christians. I know you think I'm lying, so here is a quote from their website:

### "The Southern Baptist Convention - A Closer Look

Though the discussions and information included under this category deal with important topics, they are not the most spiritually important ones. The key issue is how a person or church becomes truly Christian – anointed, Biblical, fruitful. **Not all Southern Baptists are Christians; some have proven to be nominal Christians – Christians in name only.** And not all, or even most, Christians are Southern Baptists. Countless non-Southern Baptists, and indeed, non-Baptists, have received Christ as Savior and Lord."[17]

Now that's not to pick on Southern Baptists, but it seems many non-Catholic Christians tend to share this "curiosity", and there are a few Catholics I have heard ask the same question. Are we trying to re-define the word Christian here? I guess the thing that I always wonder is who are you, I, or anyone else to question someone's faith? If someone says that they follow Christ, doesn't that make them, by definition, a Christian? It may not automatically make them a **good** Christian, but then again, who am I to judge?

Now, I hate to say it, and I know that once again I'm lip kissing a wasp nest, but I have to speak the truth here. If you are a non-Catholic Christian of *any* denomination (or non-denomination), the plain fact is that your church is either an offshoot of the Catholic Church, or an offshoot of an offshoot of the Catholic

---

[17] http://www.sbc.net/aboutus/closerlook.asp

Church. I'm perfectly happy to call you a Christian and I believe that you are one in my heart. All we as Catholics ask is the same courtesy.

Now there are a group of people who don't believe they are an offshoot of the Catholic Church, and some are those who follow the "Trail of Blood" theory. The Trail of Blood was started by Dr. J.M. Carroll of Arkansas in the early 1900's. His theory (if it can even be called that) is that his brand of non-Catholic Christian goes all the way back to Christ and that <u>they</u> and not Catholics, were the original Christians. Dr. Carroll's theory has just one small problem: there is absolutely <u>no</u> historical evidence to back him up. Apparently, according to Carroll, Jesus established a church, but mankind did not figure it out until about 100 years ago when Dr. Carroll came along!

Dr. Carroll believed that the modern day Baptist came from the Paulicians who came from the Anabaptists who came from the Montanists who claimed to be the successors of the Apostles. The first problem with that is that these groups are not linked to each other historically. Another problem for Dr. Carroll is the doctrines these beliefs had. Let's look at those for a second:

<u>Paulicians</u>- The Paulicians believed that the Evil Spirit was the author of the world, that Adam's sin was a "blessing in disguise", they rejected the entire Old Testament, and they rejected the Lord's Supper and Baptism.

Anabaptists- Believed that Christians could not bear arms, that sinners were to be excommunicated and denied the Sacraments, they believed in Apostolic succession, began "re-baptizing" adults, did not believe in going to church, but rather that people should meet and each one should preach and sing on his/her own.

Montanists- claimed direct revelations from the Holy Spirit. Its founder traveled and preached with two women who claimed to be "prophetesses" and also claimed direct revelations from the Holy Spirit; believed that those fallen from grace could never be redeemed, and they forbid remarriage.

Now those don't sound like Baptist beliefs to me, and I bet most Baptists would agree. In fact, I rarely ever see any Christian link themselves to the "Trail of Blood" theory or Dr. Carroll.

# Chapter Seven
# Papal Infallibility

## The Pope's an avocat!

*"Catholics believe that their Pope is perfect. He cannot make a mistake. They must think he is God!"*

We already touched on this one a bit, but to review, Catholics believe that, under certain circumstances, the Pope is guided by the Holy Spirit and cannot teach error. Again, not that he is impeccable (perfect). As I said before, the pope is a human and is a sinner. What we believe is that the Pope, as the Bishop of Rome, when making what we call an **BIG CATHOLIC WORD ALERT!!!** <u>ex Cathedra</u> statement (that means "from the Chair of Peter"), and he is speaking <u>on matters of faith and morals</u>, that he is guided by the Holy Spirit (as Jesus promised) and cannot err.

So where do we get this notion that the Pope is infallible under certain circumstances? Let's look at 1 John 4:6.

**1 John 4:6** *"We are of God. Whoever knows God listens to us, and he who is not of God does not listen to us. By this we know the spirit of truth and the spirit of error."*

So you will know the spirit of truth or the spirit of error, and you are either of God or not of God, by listening to or not listening to the leaders of the Church.

**Luke 10:16** *"Whoever listens to you listens to me. Whoever rejects you rejects me. And whoever rejects me rejects the one who sent me.*

Again, we either reject God or don't reject God depending upon whether or not we listen to the leaders of the Church. Now, here's Jesus speaking to the Apostles:

**Matthew 18:18** *"Amen, I say to you, whatever you bind on earth shall be bound in heaven, and whatever you loose on earth shall be loosed in heaven.*

If Jesus gave the Apostles the power to bind on earth what shall be bound in Heaven, don't you think that's pretty significant? From the time of the early Christians, this authority to bind and loose has been applied to the authority of the Church, in having the authority to pronounce on matters of faith and morals, and, as was said in Scripture, the power to forgive or retain sins (John 20). Now if in fact Jesus gave these powers to the leaders of the Church, don't you think that God probably protects them from binding or loosing error?

*"Well that's real special. What does that have to do with the Pope? I can agree that Jesus gave certain powers to the Apostles, but He didn't give any special authority to your Pope."*

Well, actually He did! And I can show you why we believe that through Scripture. I can also demonstrate to you that Jesus clearly chose a leader among the

Apostles, one to be as we call him, "first among equals".

First of all, I would like you to note that any time the names of the Apostles appear in Scripture, Peter is always mentioned first. This denotes, in that style of writing much like today who the "leader" is. Would you expect to see a statement like this: "The President and his cabinet met with....", or like this: "The cabinet and the President met with..."? The same thing applies; however, there is much more Biblical evidence than that.

Remember we just talked about the binding and loosing passage above where Jesus is speaking to the Apostles (including Peter)? Well, there is another place in the Bible where Jesus clearly gives the binding and loosing authority to Peter alone.

**Matthew 16:17-19:** *"...Blessed are you, Simon son of Jonah. For flesh and blood has not revealed this to you, but my heavenly Father. And so I say to you, you are Peter, and upon this rock I will build my church, and the gates of the netherworld shall not prevail against it. I will give you the keys to the kingdom of heaven. Whatever you bind on earth shall be bound in heaven; and whatever you loose on earth shall be loosed in heaven."*

Now a lot of stuff happened right there that you might have missed, so let's talk about it. First of all, why did Jesus call him Simon in the first sentence, but in the third sentence He calls him Peter? Well, his name was Simon. *Jesus changed Simon's name to Peter.*

Now that didn't happen often in the Bible, and the only Apostle who Jesus renamed was Peter. Now this is interesting:

God changed Abram's name to Abraham. The name Abram means "the **father** is exalted". The name Abraham means "**father** of many."

God changed Jacob's name to Israel. Jacob was the **father** to twelve sons who became ancestors to the Tribes of Israel.

God changed Simon's name to Peter. Peter became the earthly **father** of the Church.

When Jesus changed Peter's name, He made sort of a play on words. The word Peter in Aramaic is "Cephas", which means "rock". Jesus in effect said "And so I say to you, you are rock, and on this rock I will build my church..." Now you have to watch out for this argument, you will get it a lot:

*"In Greek, the word is Petros/Petras. The feminine form of the word is used, so Jesus could not have been referring to Peter when he called him 'rock'.*

This would be a brilliant argument if Jesus spoke Greek. He didn't, He spoke Aramaic. The Aramaic word is "Cephas" which is gender neutral.

Next, Jesus says to Peter "I will give you the keys to the kingdom of Heaven". Did you ever go on vacation and leave someone the keys to your house? That person is in charge of your house while you are away. The same thing happens here. Jesus leaves Peter in charge of his Church (*remember, He spoke about building the Church on Peter immediately before this sentence.*) Also, remember that Jesus says he is giving Peter *the keys to the kingdom of heaven.* These aren't just your house keys...

The only other place in Scripture where the concept of keys is used is in Isaiah 22:

**Isaiah 22:19-22** *"I will thrust you from your **office** and pull you down from your **station**. On that day I will summon my servant Eliakim, son of Hilkiah; I will clothe him with your robe, and gird him with your sash, and give over to him your **authority**. He shall be a **father** to the inhabitants of Jerusalem, and to the house of Judah. I will place the **key** of the House of David on his shoulder; **when he opens, no one shall shut, when he shuts, no one shall open.***

Well Cher, it looks to me like the keys do in fact come with authority. And, if we compare Matthew 16 to Matthew 18, here's what we get: In chapter 18, Jesus is speaking to all of the Apostles when he gives them the authority to bind and loose. In chapter 16, **Jesus is speaking to Peter alone** when he gives him the keys to the kingdom of Heaven and the authority to bind and loose. It seems pretty obvious that Peter has been set apart as a leader to the rest.

In Isaiah, the Prime Minister derives his authority from the King (who always maintains a "master key" and his own authority, just as Jesus holds the keys in Rev. 1:18; 3:7; 9:1; 20:1).

This Prime Minister is given the keys of the kingdom to "open and shut" for the King when he is not present. This same authority is given to Peter. Here's something else interesting, the people refer to the Prime Minister as "Abba" because he is a father to the people. Abba, father, daddy, papa, patriarch, pere, padre etc. are all just renditions of "father"....so is the term *Pope*.

And now you know why the Papal flag contains a picture of, guess what: *keys!*

There are also many instances in Scripture that show us that Peter was "first among equals", or what we call the "Primacy of Peter":

Peter:
Lk 22:32 - Peter's faith will strengthen his brethren
Jn 21:17 – Peter is given Christ's flock as chief shepherd
Mk 16:7 – An Angel is sent to announce the Resurrection to Peter
Lk 24:34 - The risen Jesus first appeared to Peter
Acts 1:13-26 – Peter headed the meeting which elected Matthias
Acts 2:14 – Peter led the Apostles in preaching on Pentecost
Acts 2:37-41 – Peter received the first converts
Acts 3:6-7 – Peter performed the first miracle after Pentecost
Acts 5:1-11 – Peter inflicted the first punishment: Ananias & Saphira
Acts 8:21 – Peter excommunicated the first heretic, Simon Magnus
Acts 10:44-46 – Peter received the revelation to admit Gentiles into the Church

Acts 15:7 -Peter led the first council in Jerusalem
Acts 15:19 -Peter pronounces the first dogmatic decision
Gal 1:18 - After his conversion, Paul visits the chief Apostle
Peter's name always heads the list of Apostles: Mt 10;14; Mk 3:16-19; Lk 6:14-16; Acts 1:13
Peter Spoke for the Apostles - Mt 18:21; Mk 8:29; Lk 8:45; 12:41; Jn 6:69
Acts 9:40 Peter raised Tabitha from the dead

**Peter's name occurs 195 times, more than all the rest put together.**

## Chapter Eight
## Idol Worship

**Oh Holy Stachoo, how I worship thee!**

*"Catholics bow down before and worship statues. The Bible says that we are to make no graven images, and that we are not to bow down before graven images. Look at this picture of Catholics bowing down before a statue of Mary:"*

Ok, you got me. You figured us out. The truth is that the Vatican owns a big statue company, and forces us to bow down before these statues in order to keep their sales steady.

While I was writing this chapter, I also found out something I never knew before. Not only do Catholics worship things besides God, but Protestants do too:

This is ceiling worship:

Wall worship:

Pastor worship:

And the ever popular bed worship:

This is another of those times where I will tell you that it's ok to disagree with what I as a Catholic believe. I just ask that you at least disagree with what I *actually* believe, and not what your Pastor told you I believe, what your friends told you I believe, or what you read on the internet tells you I believe. I don't believe that Protestants worship ceilings, walls, Pastors or beds. I don't make that claim because it's ridiculous. I do, however, get equally upset with the Protestant who accuses me of worshipping statues.

The first time I found out from a Protestant that I believe in worshipping statues, it came as a big surprise to me. As a kid, I attended St. Cecilia Catholic School in Broussard. As eighth graders, we were given a little more freedom and responsibility at the end of the school year. One of the things we had to do was to bring old desks up into the attic at the school. Now this is a very old school, and the attic looked like something out of a horror movie to an eighth grader: dust, cobwebs, and very dark. Anyway, a couple of us in a very dimly lit hall walked up to the doorway of a pitch black room wondering what was in it. I flicked on the light, and there standing before us was the Blessed Virgin.

No, we didn't have a Marian Apparition, it was a life-sized statue of the Virgin Mary, but it scared the pakonyad out of us. So, as good Catholic school kids, we decided that everyone else who made it to the attic should share in our fun. As another kid would come up the stairs carrying a desk, we would dare them to go into the dark room. Well, of course you can't pass up a good dare, and they would. As soon as they stepped into the room, we would give them a good push, turn on the light and lock them in the room. Now that was fun; well, until the nuns caught us. My right ear is a little longer to this day because of that incident.

The reason I'm telling you that is because when I found out that we worshipped statues, I was furious. Here you had a Catholic school, associated with a Catholic Church, and they have been keeping one of our other gods, a statue of Mary, in a dusty attic all these years.

Actually, we don't worship pieces of plaster, no matter how they are shaped. But if we did, would we put one in an attic?

Just as we don't worship Mary, neither do Catholics worship statues of Jesus, Mary or the saints. As we talked about earlier, the Catechism of the Catholic Church specifically defines idolatry:

**2113** Idolatry not only refers to false pagan worship. It remains a constant temptation to faith. Idolatry consists in divinizing what is not God. Man commits idolatry whenever he honors and reveres a creature in place of God, whether this be gods or demons (for example, satanism), power, pleasure, race, ancestors, the state, money, etc. Jesus says, "You cannot serve God and mammon." Many martyrs died for not adoring "the Beast" refusing even to simulate such worship. **Idolatry rejects the unique Lordship of God; it is therefore incompatible with communion with God.**

Now for Catholics, not being in communion with God is a really big deal. In fact, we consider idolatry a mortal sin. Now we'll talk about mortal sin later, but the name "mortal" should be enough to let you know that we believe this sin "kills" us, or rather, kills our relationship with God.

So what the heck are those Catholics doing with all those statues? Why do you see Catholics "kneeling before" a statue? Let me splain dat to you.

Does your house contain photographs of your loved ones? Do you have any photographs of a loved one who is separated from you or is possibly deceased? Have you ever caressed or kissed a photo of a loved one, or stared at that photo while reminiscing about that person? If so, I bet you are not worshipping that photo or the person in it.

We use photographs of loved ones to remember them by and as a reminder of the love we have for them. A photograph can help comfort us while a family member is away. That's exactly what Catholics do with statues and artwork. We don't worship statues any more than someone "worships" the photos in their home.

**Ex. 20:4-5:** *"You shall not make for yourself a graven image or any likeness of anything that is in heaven above, or that is in the earth beneath, or that is in the water under the earth: you shall not bow down to them or serve them."*

Uh oh. It says you can't make any graven image or any likeness of anything that is in Heaven. But wait, that means we are also in trouble if you have <u>any</u> graven image or likeness (a photograph or drawing is a likeness) of anything on earth or anything in the water. And in fact, if you are Protestant and share the view that graven images are forbidden, can we talk about the nativity scene at your church? If you have one, well, not only do you have a statue of Jesus, but you have one of Mary and St. Joseph!

Since I don't think God has a problem with the pink flamingo in my yard, let's see if we can't figure this out together, or else we are all in big trouble.

People who are against religious statues tend to "forget" about the many passages where God *commands* the making of statues.

**Ex. 25:18-20** *"And you shall make two cherubim of gold* (two gold statues of angels); *of hammered work shall you make them, on the two ends of the mercy seat. Make one cherub on the one end, and one cherub on the other end; of one piece of the mercy seat shall you make the cherubim on its two ends. The cherubim shall spread out their wings above, overshadowing the mercy seat with their wings, their faces one to another; toward the mercy seat shall the faces of the cherubim be.*

**1 Chr. 18-19:** *"...the refined gold, and its weight, to be used for the altar of incense; and, finally, gold for what would suggest a chariot throne: the cherubim that spread their wings and covered the ark of the covenant of the Lord. He had successfully committed to writing the exact specifications of the pattern, because the hand of the Lord was upon him."*

**Ezekiel 41:17-18:** *"As high as the lintel of the door, even into the interior part of the temple as well as outside, on every wall on every side in both the inner and outer rooms were carved the figures of cherubim and palmtrees: a palmtree between every two cherubim. Each cherub has two faces: a man's face looking at a palmtree on one side, and a lion's face looking at a palmtree on the other: thus they were figured on every side throughout the whole temple."*

We also see the religious use of images in Scripture. During a plague of serpents sent to punish the Israelites during the Exodus, God told Moses to *"make (a statue of) a fiery serpent, and set it on a pole; and every one who is bitten, when he sees it shall live. So Moses made a bronze serpent, and set it on a pole; and if a serpent bit any man, he would look at the bronze serpent and live"* (Num. 21:8-9).

A person had to *look* at the bronze statue of the serpent to be healed, which shows that statues could be used ritually, not just as religious decorations.

You see, God forbids the *worship* of images as gods, but He doesn't ban the making of images. If He had, religious movies, videos, photographs, paintings etc. would all be banned, as well as the Protestant 1611 King James Bible which contained pictures.

From catholic.com:

It is when people begin to adore a statue as a god that the Lord becomes angry. Thus when people *did* start to worship the bronze serpent as a snake-god (whom they named "Nehushtan"), the righteous king Hezekiah had it destroyed

(2Kgs.18:4).[18]

**Bow yousef down before me.**

*"In Deuteronomy 5:9, concerning idols, God said "You shall not bow down to them. Catholics 'bow down' to these images."*

Many Catholics sometimes bow or kneel in front of statues of Jesus and the saints. Anti-Catholics confuse this with the sin of idolatry.

"Bowing can be used as a posture in worship, but not all bowing is worship. In Japan, people show respect by bowing in greeting. A person can kneel before a king without worshipping him as a god. In the same way, a Catholic who may kneel in front of a statue while praying isn't worshipping the statue or even praying to *it*, any more than the Protestant who kneels with a Bible in his hands when praying is worshipping the Bible or praying to *it*."[19]

And of course, you know the Catholic Church had itself a council. The Second Council of Nicaea (787), which dealt largely with the question of the religious use of images and icons, said,

"[T]he one who redeemed us from the darkness of idolatrous insanity, Christ our God, when he took for his bride his holy Catholic Church . . . promised he would guard her and assured his holy disciples saying, 'I am with you every day until the consummation of this age.' . . . To this gracious offer some people paid no attention; being hoodwinked by the treacherous foe they abandoned the true line of reasoning . .

---

[18] Catholic Answers, *"Do Catholics Worship Statues?"*, (San Diego, Catholic Answers, 2004)
[19] Ibid.

**. and they failed to distinguish the holy from the profane, asserting that the icons of our Lord and of his saints were no different from the wooden images of satanic idols."**

The *Catechism of the Council of Trent* (1566) taught that idolatry is committed "by worshipping idols and images as God, or believing that they possess any divinity or virtue entitling them to our worship, by praying to, or reposing confidence in them".

And from the Catechism of the Catholic Church:

"Idolatry is a perversion of man's innate religious sense. An idolater is someone who 'transfers his indestructible notion of God to anything other than God'"

And from Catholic Answers:

"The Catholic Church absolutely recognizes and condemns the sin of idolatry. What anti-Catholics can't see is the difference between thinking a piece of plaster is a god and using that image to help us remember and contemplate God and the saints. The making and use of religious statues is a *thoroughly* biblical practice. Anyone who says otherwise doesn't know his Bible."[20]

---

[20] Catholic Answers, "*Do Catholics Worship Statues?*", (San Diego, Catholic Answers, 2004)

## Chapter Nine
## Purgatory

*"Catholics believe in a place called 'Purgatory'. They believe that when you die, you don't go straight to Heaven, but that you are punished in Purgatory. This is another man-made belief which was invented by Catholics so they could raise money by selling indulgences."*

Unfortunately, Protestants have a hard time understanding Purgatory because they do not allow for man to play a part in his own salvation. "Jesus does it all". They also often tend to link Purgatory with the selling of indulgences during the Reformation. Let's get the selling of indulgences part out of the way first, then we can talk about Purgatory. A couple of definitions may help at this point:

Temporal punishment- Catholics believe that there is a punishment related to sin. For each sin you commit, in a sense, you have to pay for it later, even if the sin has been forgiven by way of Confession. I'll give you an analogy. Suppose you are playing baseball as a kid, and you hit the ball through the neighbor's window. You can go over and apologize to the neighbor and be forgiven, and you are. The window, though, is still broken. The situation has not returned to the way it was until you pay for the window or go fix it yourself. That's the *temporal punishment*. Catholics believe the same applies to sin. We have to pay for them either in this world or in the next.

Indulgence-An indulgence, the Catholic Church teaches, is one of the ways you can "fix the window" with God. It is usually some action, such as reading the Bible, which the Church defines as one of the ways to pay for what you have done. Now there are indulgences which only partially fix the window and we call those *partial indulgences*. (I know what you're thinking; the Church couldn't come up with a bigger word, or at least a Latin one?) Another kind of indulgence removes all of the temporal punishment of sin, and we call those *plenary indulgences*.

So what happened during the reformation is that there were some of the clergy who started selling indulgences like it was a fundraiser or something. Instead of having a KC Jambalaya or a bake sale, they would sell indulgences. Now that is a really, really bad thing to do.

For instance, my church has a building fund to pay for additions, etc. Now if Father Louis were to tell the parishioners, "If you give ten bucks to the church, you get a partial indulgence, and if you give twenty bucks you get a plenary indulgence"; that would be a big old whopping sin. The Catholic Church calls that the sin of Simony.

There was this fella in the Bible named Simon the Magician who saw the Apostles doing miracles. He wanted the same power for himself, so he offered to pay Peter so he could be granted this power. Well let me tell you, Peter lit into him like you would not believe. He was on Simon like white on rice. It was so bad in fact, that poor Simon the Magician wound up begging Peter to pray for him to God to make things right. Now you know how the sin of Simony got its name. Read all about it in Acts 8:9-25.

Now Simony is wrong, and the Catholic Church has always taught that it's wrong. There were a few of the clergy during the reformation who did it anyway, and people are still complaining to this day.

So, now you know what an indulgence is and sort of how it is linked to Purgatory. You also know that selling indulgences is wrong. Since we got all of that out of the way, let's get back to what this chapter is supposed to be about: Purgatory.

First of all, you need to understand that Purgatory is not necessarily a *place*, but rather a *state of being*. Now can we find the concept of Purgatory in the Bible? You bet your biggest cast iron pot you can!

**Matthew 12:32:** *"And whoever speaks a word against the Son of Man will be forgiven; but whoever speaks against the holy Spirit **will not be forgiven, either in this age or in the age to come.**"*

Well, that tells me that some sins can be forgiven *in the age to come*. Now it can't be Heaven, because there isn't any sin in Heaven. It can't be Hell, because there's no more chance for forgiveness in Hell, and it's permanent. So there must be another place.....

**1 Corinthians 3:15** *"But if someone's work is burned up, that one will suffer loss; **the person will be saved, but only as through fire.**"*

What? **The person will be saved, but only as through fire?** So there's some way, like with fire, that we are saved? Well, that again cannot mean either Heaven or Hell as we just talked about. But what's with the "as through fire" part?

**Zechariah 13:8-9:** *"In all the land says the Lord, two thirds of them shall be cut off and perish, and one third shall be left. I will bring the one third through fire, and <u>I will refine them as silver is refined</u>, and I will test them as gold is tested..."*

When a silversmith refines silver, he **heats** it to purify it. The silversmith has to carefully watch the silver during this process because if he heats it for too long, it will be destroyed. There is the story of a woman who was contemplating this passage, and who went to watch a silversmith work. She asked him, "How do you know when the silver is pure?" The silversmith answered "Easy. *When I can see my image in it."*

**1 Peter 3:18-20** *"For Christ also suffered for sins once, the righteous for the sake of the unrighteous, that he might lead you to God. Put to death in the flesh, he was brought to life in the spirit. In it **he also went to preach to the spirits in prison**, who had once been disobedient while God patiently waited in the days of Noah during the building of the ark, in which a few persons, eight in all, were saved through water.*

Spirits in prison?

**1 Peter 4:6** *"For this is why the gospel was preached even to the dead that, though condemned in the flesh <u>in human estimation</u>, they might live in the spirit in the estimation of God.*

So there's a prison for disobedient spirits, yet they were saved when Jesus preached to them. Well then where is this prison? Scripture doesn't tell us, but it makes it clear that there is a place besides Heaven and Hell. Believing there is only Heaven or Hell is **not** Scriptural:

**2 Maccabees 12:44-46** *"...for if he were not expecting the fallen to rise again, it would have been useless and foolish to pray for them in death. But if he did this with a view to the splendid reward that awaits those who had gone to rest in godliness, it was a holy and pious thought."*

What happened here was that Judas (not the Apostle) and his men went to collect the dead on the battlefield to bury them. Under their tunics were found types of amulets which were forbidden under the law. These men were slain because they were practicing idolatry. So Judas took up a collection from his men and basically made a donation to help their sin be forgiven. This passage, once again, shows us that there is a way by which sin can be forgiven after death.

Now we know that Jesus and the Apostles were Jews, so what was the Jewish take on prayers for the dead? *The Mourner's Kaddish* is a Jewish prayer for the deceased person's soul. I found this note from a Jewish man who was helping make the point that the Catholic idea of Purgatory is similar to Jewish belief:

"Our prayer, the Mourner's Kaddish, is for the benefit of the soul of the deceased & is believed to ease the spiritual status of the deceased's soul as it goes through whatever trials & tribulations it may be subject to. Yes, we do believe in something akin to the Roman Catholic notion of Purgatory & thus saying the Mourner's Kaddish would be similar to the Roman Catholic idea of praying for the souls in Purgatory.
In addition to the Kaddish. it is believed that the recitation of the Yizkor and E-l Maleh Rahamim prayers are beneficial to the soul of the departed. On the anniversary of the burial, it is common to study some chapter of the Talmud or the Tanakh (what we Christians call the "Old Testament"), read a selection of Psalms, give to charity, etc. in honor/memory of the departed. This is also believed to be beneficial." [21]

So you see, the concept of Purgatory is ancient. The denial of Purgatory is itself a modern man-made belief.

Now let's use common sense:

-Can something that is impure, or more to the point, can a soul, enter Heaven stained with sin? No. We can all agree on that.

-What happens to a person who dies stained with sin but who is still good enough to make it to Heaven? There must be some process by which the soul is cleansed, or purified, or purged. Catholics call that Purgatory!

---

[21] http://blackieschurchmilitant-apocalypsis.blogspot.com/2007/06/biblical-and-jewish-traditional-beliefs.html

# Chapter Ten
# Lagniappe

In Cajun French, there's a term we use called "Lagniappe". Lagniappe means "a little something extra", and that's what this chapter is; all the miscellaneous stuff I didn't think should be put in its own chapter.

**The Piccadilly is open!**

Ok, this one is for the Catholics only. You know, it's hard enough to defend our faith without having to hear *"Well, I know plenty of Catholics who don't agree with the Church's teaching on…"*

I know that the Catholics reading this agree with most of the teachings they have read about here, but I have to say, there are maybe some beliefs in the Church that you don't agree with and don't follow. If so, you are what is called a "Cafeteria Catholic". You go through the cafeteria line of Church dogma and just take the ones you want and leave the rest. Now let me say this, and I know I'm gonna offend a bunch of you, but dang it, it don't work that way.

In other faiths, there are things you can disagree with and be perfectly ok. Of course, there are certain beliefs in Protestantism also that you cannot disagree with if you are a true Protestant. If, for instance, you are Lutheran or Baptist or of any other Protestant faith, you can't claim that Jesus is not God and still be of that faith. It just don't work that way.

Well, the same applies to Catholicism. I know there are those of you out there who disagree with Church teaching on things like annulments or birth control or whatever, but you have to remember that Christ established this Church, and He promised to guide it and to be with it forever. So, if something is declared to be a doctrine of the Church, as a Catholic, you have to follow it. There ain't no wiggle room here.

If you are from this area, you probably vacation in Destin, Florida sometimes. If so, I know you have been to Corpus Christi Catholic Church on Beach Drive, right? You do go to Mass when you're on vacation, don't you? We'll leave that one alone for now. Anyway, I attended Mass there recently and heard a great homily by Father Robert Morris.

Father Morris was talking about this very issue, (and I'll try to quote him as well as I can remember here) and he said "You cannot be in favor of abortion and call yourself a Catholic. If you do, that makes you a liar."

Father Morris is tough, but he is absolutely right, and I'm glad he said it. The same principle holds true with other dogmas of the Church. Here's a quote from an Early Church Father which addresses this issue:

"Whence you ought to know that the bishop is in the Church, and the Church in the bishop; **and if any one be not with the bishop, that he is not in the Church**, and that those flatter themselves in vain who creep in, not having peace with God's priests, and think that they communicate secretly with some; while **the Church, which is Catholic and one, is not cut nor divided**, but is indeed connected and bound together by the cement of priests who cohere with one another." *Cyprian, To Florentius, Epistle 66/67 (A.D. 254).*

Now I know some of you may be separated from the Church over one of these issues, and some of you are hurting because of that separation, but there is ALWAYS a way home. Talk to your priest. If that's your situation, we would love to have you back and your priest can tell you what you need to do. We miss you.

## Annulments

*"I'm not Catholic anymore. I got married at a young age. For a while, everything was fine, but later, my husband changed. He became violent and abusive. Long story short, I left him and sometime later I met a man whom I dearly love. We were married outside the Church, have three kids together, and are all very happy. I can't marry in the Catholic Church, so I have just moved on. What gives a priest the right to tell me that I can't get married? Apparently I have to go through this long process, and of course, pay the Church a bunch of money just to get permission to marry again. I think the whole process is just a money making deal."*

No matter how you slice it, divorce is ugly. Many people think the Church has an overly strict view on marriage. Why is that? Well, once again, the Church has proven faithful to the teachings of Christ. Now we all like to hear parts of the following passage at a wedding, but not too many people want to hear it when talking about divorce:

**Matthew 19:3-9:** *"Some Pharisees approached him, and tested him, saying, 'Is it lawful for a man to divorce his wife for any cause whatever?' He said in reply, 'Have you not read that from the beginning the Creator made them male and female and said, 'For this reason a man shall leave his father and mother and be joined to his wife, and the two shall become one flesh?' So they are no longer two, but one flesh. Therefore, what God has joined together, no human being must separate.' They said to him, 'Then why did Moses command that the man give the woman a bill of divorce and dismiss her?' He said to them, 'Because of the hardness of your hearts Moses allowed you to divorce your wives, but from the beginning it was not so.* **I say to you, whoever divorces his wife (unless the marriage is unlawful) and marries another commits adultery."**

So here we have Jesus Himself telling us that once two people are married, they are joined *by God.* So man better not be undoing what God has done. All the Catholic Church does with respect to marriage is to take God at His word.

*"Well, isn't that exactly what the Church does in an annulment? Undo what God has done?"*

Nope. What the Church does in an annulment is to investigate and declare in certain circumstances that *a valid marriage did not exist in the first place.* The Church is not granting a religious divorce!

Here's a for instance for you. Suppose a 35 year old man marries a ten year old girl. Would you consider that a valid marriage, either civilly or religiously? Of course not. A ten year old cannot make an informed adult decision.

What the Catholic Church has done is to specifically define what conditions exist that nullify a marriage, that is, declare that it never happened in the first place because of some defect. There are several defects that can make a marriage invalid, so it's best to talk to your priest if you would like the Bishop to consider the validity of your marriage.

You should understand, however, that your priest cannot grant an annulment. He can help you to get the ball rolling, but annulment questions go before the Diocesan Tribunal, and that's where the money part comes in. There are a large number of annulments before the Tribunal at any one given time, and that's one of the things that cause an annulment to take so long. The Church asks you to pay a portion of their cost to investigate the marriage. The Tribunal will often hire subject matter experts to help them investigate an individual case. For instance, if a person claims that one of the parties in a marriage was mentally incompetent at the time, the Tribunal may decide to hire a psychiatrist.

The Tribunal will also interview witnesses and do other research. All of this takes time and money. Due to these costs, the Diocese is not realizing any substantive money on annulments. Now you should also know that there is a process to have the annulment fee reduced or waived if someone does not have the ability to pay. No person is ever denied access to the Tribunal due to lack of funds.

Here's something interesting: Most of the Protestant churches I researched have a prohibition of one sort or another against divorce and remarriage. This is from the Southern Baptist Convention's Resolution on Divorce:

"WHEREAS, The facility with which divorces are at present obtained in our courts is an incentive to exaggerate the minor difficulties of married life, and an encouragement to dissolve the union that otherwise would continue with difficulties removed and

WHEREAS, The laws of our States, with a few exceptions, permit divorces for many and often trivial cases; therefore

RESOLVED, That it is the sense of this body that the Legislatures of the States represented in this Convention be requested to discourage this great and growing evil by more stringent laws regulating the same.

**RESOLVED, That it is the sense of this body that Baptist ministers should refuse to solemnize the rites of matrimony in cases where one or both parties concerned have been divorced on other than Scriptural grounds, as laid down in Matthew 19:9."[22]**

So don't just blame the Catholic Church. Like many other Christian churches, we are just following what Jesus said! You see, in the Southern Baptist Convention's resolution on divorce, they cite Matthew 19:9. The problem is, though, that they don't define what those Scriptural grounds are that would nullify a marriage. So the question remains, how do they determine whether or not a marriage was "Scriptural" in the first place?

---

[22] Southern Baptist Convention, *Resolution on Divorce,*
http://www.sbc.net/resolutions/amResolution.asp?ID=441

**It's Lent... Let's fry some fish!**

I'm going to direct this first part to the Catholics, then we will look at why we fast/abstain during Lent and certain holy days.

Ok, for the Catholics: Many Protestants laugh at this practice, and y'all know better! Do you honestly think that God appreciates you skipping the ham sandwich on Fridays during lent so you can share in Jesus' agony by eating a seafood platter? Do you feel the pain He endured while at that crawfish boil? Does that fried catfish help you contemplate how the spikes felt as they were nailed through His hands and feet?

Do I have you feeling a little bit guilty? Good. Now, just so you know, I do the same thing every now and then, because it's really hard to pass up a crawfish boil, and after all, God wouldn't want us to waste crawfish now would He? I guess you and I both should probably stop and think a bit of what's actually asked of us here, and in the future, maybe we can plan a bit better for Lenten Fridays. Maybe we can all work a little harder for Him too. Want to really get into the spirit of Lenten Fridays? Try a bread and water fast for the day. Trust me, that will keep your head where it belongs.

**Matthew 9:15:** *"...The days will come when the bridegroom is taken away from them, and then they will fast."*

All through the Bible we hear talk of "prayer and fasting". Jesus Himself fasted. If it's good for Jesus to do, and we are told over and over again to do it, we should probably fast too, right? There are some days the Church tells us we are to fast, and some days that we are to both fast and abstain. What dat means?

**Fasting**, according to the Catechism is "Refraining from food and drink as an expression of interior penance, in imitation of the fast of Jesus for forty days in the desert."

**Abstinence** is completely giving something up, in this case, certain foods.

Fasting is only required on Ash Wednesday and Good Friday. This consists of one full meal at most, and two other small meals that combined do not equal another full meal. You may drink water throughout the day, but you should remember that **one of the purposes of fasting is to feel hunger.**

Abstinence from meat is required on Ash Wednesday, Good Friday, and the other Fridays in Lent. And before you ask, chicken is meat. We can eat fish, but you should realize that this is actually a relaxing of the discipline because y'all were pouting so much.

Now the whole purpose of fasting and abstinence is to suffer a little so that we remember how Christ suffered for us. The intention was never for us to have fried shrimp for God. In fact, in doing research for this book, I found the real reason that we give up meat on Fridays during Lent.

In the early Church, they wanted Christians to partake in a more personal way in Christ's crucifixion, and thought that it would spiritually benefit people to, in a small way, "feel the pain" that Christ felt. Catholic monks began experimenting with certain foods to further this objective. They were looking for some food which would help Catholics really remember the Passion. They began experimenting with certain types of seafood because the idea was that when the faithful gave up meat, they would then eat something else, in this case seafood.

After much testing, the monks found they could grind a mixture of things and compress them to make a patty. The patty would then be fried. The mixture they settled upon consisted of the European version of a choupique, shrimp peelings, and what we call a marsh hen. The mixture was ground, formed into a square patty and fried in cod liver oil.[23]

The Church thought this would really catch on, so they made millions of these patties. The problem was, the early Christians thought this was too much, and largely abandoned the practice of eating these. Not willing to waste food, the Church then began distributing these patties to Catholic schools. They became known as the "Catholic School Friday Fish Patty". I have it on good authority that these patties exist to this day, and continue to be served in Catholic school cafeterias all over the country.

---

[23] It's really neat that you, *read the footnotes*, but this one won't take you anywhere, (because I made it all up in, 2009, Broussard, La., all rights reserved).

Ok, I admit it. I made all of that up, but I had you going for a minute. Honestly, have you ever eaten one of those? That's penance right there.

I'll close this section with a quote because it comes from an Early Church Father, it mentions this practice, and it's pretty funny:

"For what does it profit if we abstain from fish and fowl and yet bite and devour our brothers and sisters? The evil speaker eats the flesh of his brother and bites the body of his neighbor."
St. John Chrysostom

**No Bible for you!**

*"The Catholic Church claims it is a Bible-believing church, yet this same Church banned the Bible at one time! In 1229, the Bible was forbidden to laymen and placed on the Index of Forbidden Books by the Council of Valencia."*

If you really want to get yourself tied up in a knot, you should read the anti-Catholic book *Roman Catholicism* by Loraine Boettner. It's about as wildly inaccurate as anything I have ever read. The idea above came from that book, and unfortunately anti-Catholics still like to use it without ever doing any research into its validity.

First of all, there was no Council of Valencia that I could find. Also, the Moors were in control of that area in 1229, so it would have been "uncomfortable", or rather deadly, to have a council there. Instead, I guess

Boettner may have meant the Council of Toulouse, since it was held in 1229.

Now the Council of Toulouse was called because there was a heresy going around called the Albigensian/Manichean heresy. Ever since the establishment of the Church, there have been all sorts of heresies running around, and the Church always gets together to fight them off. The folks who were part of this heresy believed that the flesh is evil and therefore marriage is evil, fornication is not a sin, and suicide is not immoral.

The Albigensians were using a corrupt version of the Bible to support their strange theories, and were twisting the Bible to prove their point. So to fight this, the Bishops at Toulouse restricted the use of the Bible until this heresy was ended. When the heresy ended, the restriction was lifted. Now the Council of Toulouse was a regional council, not an ecumenical council, so it did not have authority on the Church as a whole. The restriction never affected more than one area of Southern France, so it's a far cry from the Catholic Church banning the Bible from all laymen.

Also there were *certain translations* of the Bible on the Index of Forbidden Books, not because they were Bibles, but because they were corrupt Bibles with altered text reflecting heretical views. Since Protestants must admit that only the Catholic Church had the Bible for the first 1500 years after Christ's death, they should appreciate the fact that the Catholic Church went to such great lengths to preserve its integrity.

A Protestant once used the same attack on a Catholic apologetics forum as Boettner did. One of the apologists asked him this question:

"Do you allow your family whom you love to use a Jehovah's Witness Bible for their study? I think not. Then the same thing is true of the Church in dealing with gross errors in vernacular translations."

**Wine or Welch's?**

*"We use grape juice and not wine when we celebrate the Lord's Supper because that is what was used by Jesus and the Apostles."*

I probably should not have even included this one, because I think most Protestants probably know it is not true, but since some continue to make this argument, I thought I would just touch on it briefly.

So here we are again with (some) Protestants using the literalist interpretation of the Bible unless it doesn't suit their beliefs. What does the Bible say, wine or grape juice? Some say the word "wine" actually refers to grape juice.

Here's the problem: during the time of year that the Last Supper was held, the grape harvest season was long over. There was no pasteurization in those days, and of course they didn't have refrigerators, so the only thing that could have been used at the Last Supper was wine. Grape juice would have been rotten (or, turned into wine on its own). And, once again, if the Bible is actually referring to grape juice, why didn't it just say grape juice instead?

And what about all those passages that refer to someone getting drunk by drinking too much wine? Did you ever hear of someone getting drunk from too much grape juice? Jesus not only turned water into wine, but He drank wine and at one point was accused of being a drunkard (Luke 7:34).

**Real Bad Sin and Just Regular Sin**

There are some Protestants who do not believe in the concept of mortal sin. The Catholic Church teaches that there is a type of sin that "kills" our relationship with God unless we repent. We call that mortal sin. The concept of mortal sin has been a constant belief in Christianity since the very beginning.

"It was not until the time of John Calvin that anyone would claim that it was impossible for a true Christian to lose his salvation. That teaching, which was not even shared by Martin Luther and his followers, was a theological novelty of the mid-sixteenth century, a teaching which would have been condemned as a *dangerous heresy* by all previous generations of Christians. **It would drive people to the despair of thinking that, if they had committed grave sins, they had never been true Christians.** Further, they would suffer similar anxiety over any subsequent conversion, since their first would not have been genuine, according to this teaching. **Or it would drive them into thinking that their grave sins were really *not* grave at all, for no true Christian could have committed such sins.**

**In time the "once saved, always saved" teaching even degenerated in many Evangelical circles to the point that some would claim that a Christian *could* commit**

**grave sins and still remain saved: sin did not injure his relationship with God at all."[24]**

"The Catholic Church shares the belief in mortal sin with the Eastern Orthodox, Lutheran, Anglican, Methodist, and Pentecostal churches. Only Presbyterians, Baptists and those who have been influenced by these two sects reject the reality of mortal sin."[25]

Why do you think that John Calvin and some of the other Protestants don't like the concept of mortal sin? Obviously, it simply cannot fit in with the "Once Saved, Always Saved" belief. If a person is saved, and that salvation is permanent, how can you explain a type of sin that "kills" our relationship with God? So where do we get our belief in mortal sin? Let's start with the Bible.

**1 John 5:16-17** *If anyone sees his brother sinning, if the sin is not deadly, he should pray to God and he will give him life. This is only for those whose sin is not deadly. There is such a thing as deadly sin, about which I do not say that you should pray. All wrongdoing is sin, but there is sin that is not deadly.*

This passage makes it obvious that there are two types of sin: one which is deadly, and one which is not deadly. It also explains why the Catholic Church teaches that we are to confess our mortal sins to a priest (although the Church recommends you confess venial sins also).

---

[24] Catholic Answers, *"Mortal Sin"*, (San Diego: Catholic Answers, 2004)

[25] Catholic Answers, *"Mortal Sin"*, (San Diego: Catholic Answers, 2004)

The passage says that if a sin is not deadly, we should pray to God and be forgiven, but if the sin is deadly, we should not pray. Well then, what do we do with that "deadly" sin? God forgives it through the Sacrament of Reconciliation!

## "What dem old people said?"

The Early Church Fathers were unanimous in their teaching of mortal sin.

**"Tertullian** "Discipline governs a man, power sets a seal upon him; apart from the fact that power is the Spirit, but the Spirit is God. What, moreover, used [the Spirit] to teach? That there must be no communicating with the works of darkness. Observe what he bids. Who, moreover, was able to forgive sins? This is his alone prerogative: for 'who remits sins but God alone?' and, of course, [who but he can remit] mortal sins, such as have been committed against himself and against his temple?" (*Modesty* 21 [A.D. 220]).

**Basil the Great** "The clergyman who is deposed for mortal sin shall not be excommunicated" (*Canonical Letter,* canon 32 [A.D. 374]).

**Pacian of Barcelona** "Stinginess is remedied by generosity, insult by apology, perversity by honesty, and for whatever else, amends can be made by practice of the opposite. But what can he do who is contemptuous of God? What shall the murderer do? What remedy shall the fornicator find? . . . These are capital sins, brethren, these are mortal. Someone may say: 'Are we then about to perish? . . . Are we to die in our sins?' . . . I appeal first to you brethren who refuse penance for your acknowledged crimes. You, I say, who are timid after your impudence, who are bashful after your sins, who are not ashamed to sin but now are ashamed to confess" (*Sermon Exhorting to Penance* 4 [A.D. 385]).

**Jerome** "There are venial sins and there are mortal sins. It is one thing to owe ten thousand talents, another to owe but a farthing. We shall have to give an accounting for an idle word no less than for adultery. But to be made to blush and to be tortured are not the same thing; not the same thing to grow red in the face and to be in agony for a long time. . . . If we entreat for lesser sins we are granted pardon, but for greater sins, it is difficult to obtain our request. There is a great difference between one sin and another" (*Against Jovinian* 2:30 [A.D. 393])."[26]

Now occasionally Catholics may forget some things about mortal sin, so let's review real quick. There are three conditions that have to be met for a sin to be mortal:

1- It must be grave (really bad) matter.

2) You have to know it is wrong. The Ten Commandments tell us many things that are wrong, and so do other parts of Scripture.

3) You have to do it willfully. So for example, punching someone in the mouth is willful. Killing someone in a car accident is not.

If you want to know whether or not something is a mortal sin, the best place to start is the Catechism. One big thing for all you Catholics to remember is that *you cannot receive Communion if you are stained with mortal sin.* Receiving Communion while guilty of mortal sin is another mortal sin. Now would be a good

---

[26] Catholic Answers, *"Mortal Sin"*, (San Diego: Catholic Answers, 2004)

time for you to remember in Chapter Three where we quoted this passage:

**I Corinthians 11:27**: *"Therefore whoever eats the bread or drinks the cup of the Lord unworthily will have to answer for the body and blood of the Lord."*

**The Rosary**

The word Rosary comes from Latin and means a garland of roses, the rose being one of the flowers used to symbolize the Virgin Mary. Well, we get criticized for praying the Rosary too, so we'd better talk about that. First of all, where did the Rosary come from?

"It's commonly said that St. Dominic, the founder of the Order of Preachers (the Dominicans), instituted the rosary. Not so. Certain parts of the rosary predated Dominic; others arose only after his death.

Centuries before Dominic, monks had begun to recite all 150 psalms on a regular basis. As time went on, it was felt that the lay brothers, known as the *conversi*, should have some form of prayer of their own. They were distinct from the choir monks, and a chief distinction was that they were illiterate. Since they couldn't read the psalms, they couldn't recite them with the monks. They needed an easily remembered prayer.

The prayer first chosen was the Our Father, and, depending on circumstances, it was said either fifty or a hundred times. These *conversi* used rosaries to keep count, and the rosaries were known then as *Paternosters* ("Our Fathers").

In England there arose a craftsmen's guild of some importance, the members of which made these rosaries. In London you can find a street, named Paternoster Row, which preserves the memory of the area where these craftsmen worked.

The rosaries that originally were used to count Our Fathers came to be used, during the twelfth century, to count Hail Marys—or, more properly, the first half of what we now call the Hail Mary. (The second half was added some time later.)

Both Catholics and non-Catholics, as they learn more about the rosary and make more frequent use of it, come to see how its meditations bring to mind the sweet fragrance not only of the Mother of God, but of Christ himself."[27]

So that's a little history for you, but what about accusations made against Catholics and the Rosary by some Protestants?

*"Catholics pray the rosary which is the same prayers repeated over and over again. This is in direct contradiction to Matthew 6:7 which warns against repetitive prayer."*

Actually, the warning is against "vain and repetitive prayer", depending on the Bible version you use. I don't think we can call the prayers of the Rosary "vain", unless you think Scripture is vain. What Jesus was warning against here was the "babbling" type of prayer of the Pagans, who thought that basically the more words you used, the better. So what of the Protestant charge that repetitive prayer is forbidden?

Maybe these critics never read Psalm 136, or other Scriptural prayer which use repetition.

---

[27] Catholic Answers *"The Rosary"*, (San Diego: Catholic Answers, 2004)

**Psalm 136:**
*Praise the Lord, who is so good;*
*God's love endures forever;*
*Praise the God of gods;*
*God's love endures forever;*
*Praise the Lord of lords;*
*God's love endures forever;*

*Who alone has done great wonders,*
*God's love endures forever;*
*Who skillfully made the heavens,*
*God's love endures forever;*
*Who spread the earth upon the waters,*
*God's love endures forever;*
*Who made the great lights,*
*God's love endures forever;*
*The sun to rule the day,*
*God's love endures forever;*
*The moon and stars to rule the night,*
*God's love endures forever;*

*Who struck down the firstborn of Egypt,*
*God's love endures forever;*
*And led Israel from their midst,*
*God's love endures forever;*
*With mighty hand and outstretched arm,*
*God's love endures forever;*
*Who split in two the Red Sea,*
*God's love endures forever;*
*And led Israel through,*
*God's love endures forever;*
*But swept Pharaoh and his army into the Red Sea,*
*God's love endures forever;*

It goes on from there, but you get the point. The other point is that this Psalm was meant to be sung in a Jewish Temple. It was a form of repetitive prayer. What critics of the Rosary fail to understand is that the Rosary is a meditative prayer. When Catholics recite the Rosary, we reflect on various parts of Scripture:

**The Joyful Mysteries** (Monday and Saturday)
The Annunciation (Luke 1:26-38),
The Visitation (Luke 1:40-56),
The Nativity (Luke 2:6-20),
The Presentation of Jesus in the Temple (Luke 2:21-39),
The Finding of the child Jesus in the Temple (Luke 2:41-51).

**The Sorrowful Mysteries** (Tuesday and Friday)
The Agony in the Garden (Matt. 26:36-46),
The Scourging (Matt. 27:26),
The Crowning with Thorns (Matt. 27:29),
The Carrying of the Cross (John 19:17),
The Crucifixion (Luke 23:33-46).

**The Luminous Mysteries** (Thursday)
The Baptism of Christ (Matthew 4:13-17)
The Wedding Feast at Cana (John 2:1-12)
The Announcement of the Kingdom (Mark 1:15)
The Transfiguration (Luke 9:28-36)
The Institution of the Eucharist (John 6:22-71)

**The Glorious Mysteries** (Wednesday and Sunday)
The Resurrection (Luke 24:1-12),
The Ascension (Luke 24:50-51),
The Descent of the Holy Spirit (Acts 2:1-4),

The Assumption of Mary (Rev. 12),
The Coronation of Mary (cf. Rev. 12:1).

The last two are not explicitly Scriptural, but they aren't contrary to Scripture either, so there is no reason to reject them since they come from the teaching authority of the Church. Guess what? Many Protestants, once they understand what the rosary is all about, take up the practice of this devotion.

**Father don't know, he's not married.**

*"Catholic Priests cannot marry. That's probably why so many of them become child molesters."*

No, I didn't quote that one just to tick off the Catholics. That is actually a charge that is sometimes heard from Protestants, and I am quoting that statement by an anti-Catholic on an apologetics forum. Can't you just feel the Christian love? The above statement presumes that a person who lives a celibate life will almost certainly become a sexual deviant. I don't think it's really necessary to respond to that attack, but if it were true, I suppose there wouldn't be any *married* sexual deviants at all, right? Now that we got that ridiculous statement out of the way, let's talk about Priestly celibacy.

First of all, priestly celibacy is not a dogma or doctrine of the Church, but a *discipline*. Priestly celibacy is not a rule for all Catholic priests, and some are, in fact, married. In fact, for Eastern Rite Catholics, married priests are the *norm*, just as they are for

Orthodox and Oriental Christians.[28] In the Eastern churches, there have always been some restrictions on marriage and ordination. A married man may become a priest, but unmarried priests cannot marry, and married priests, if widowed, cannot remarry.

"In the Western (Latin-Rite) Church, the tradition has been for priests and bishops to take vows of celibacy since the early Middle Ages. Even today, though, there are exceptions. For example, there are married Latin-Rite priests who are converts from Lutheranism and Episcopalianism."[29]

Is there Scriptural support for priestly celibacy? You bet!

**1 Corinthians 7:8-9:** *"Now to the unmarried and to widows I say: it is a good thing for them to remain as they are, as I do, but if they cannot exercise self-control they should marry, for it is better to marry than to be on fire."*

**1 Corinthians 7:27-34** *"Are you free from a wife? Do not seek marriage. . . those who marry will have worldly troubles, and I would spare you that. . . . The unmarried man is anxious about the affairs of the Lord, how to please the Lord; but the married man is anxious about worldly affairs, how to please his wife, and his interests are divided. And the unmarried woman or girl is anxious about the affairs of the Lord, how to be holy*

---

[28] Catholic Answers, *"Celibacy and the Priesthood"*, (San Diego: Catholic Answers, 2004)
[29] Ibid.

*in body and spirit; but the married woman is anxious about worldly affairs, how to please her husband".*

**Matthew 19:11-12***: "Not all can accept this word, but only those to whom it is granted. Some are incapable of marriage because they were born so; some, because they were made so by others;* **some, because they have renounced marriage for the sake of the kingdom of God. Whoever can accept this ought to accept it".*

"Notice that this sort of celibacy "for the sake of the kingdom" is a gift, a call that is not granted to all, or even most people, but is granted to some. Other people are called to marriage. It is true that too often individuals in both vocations fall short of the requirements of their state, but this does not diminish either vocation, nor does it mean that the individuals in question were "not really called" to that vocation. The sin of a priest doesn't necessarily prove that he never should have taken a vow of celibacy, any more than the sin of a married man or woman proves that he or she never should have gotten married. It is possible for us to fall short of our own true calling.

Celibacy is neither unnatural nor unbiblical. "Be fruitful and multiply" is not binding upon every individual; rather, it is a general precept for the human race. Otherwise, every unmarried man and woman of marrying age would be in a state of sin by remaining single, and Jesus and Paul would be guilty of advocating sin as well as committing it."[30]

---

[30] Catholic Answers, *"Celibacy and the Priesthood"*, (San Diego: Catholic Answers, 2004)

## The Whore of Babylon

*"For anyone who reads the Book of Revelation, chapter 17, it is obvious that the 'Whore of Babylon' is in fact, the Roman Catholic Church. The whore is a city built on seven hills. Ancient Rome is built on seven hills. The woman is called a whore with whom early kings have committed fornication. The Vatican has entered into unholy alliances with other nations and kingdoms. "She [the Whore] is clothed in 'purple and scarlet' (verse 4), the colors of the Catholic clergy. In his vision, John notes the great wealth of the whore, 'decked with gold and precious stones and pearls'. One should note the great wealth that the Catholic Church possesses. The Whore has 'a golden cup [chalice] in her hand, full of abominations and filthiness of her fornication.'" This is another reference to Revelation 17:4. The Catholic Church is known for its many thousands of gold chalices around the world. John next notices that the woman is drunk—not with alcohol but with the blood of the saints, and with the blood of the martyrs of Jesus . . . [cf. verse 6]. One here should note the brutality and killing by the Inquisitions, the forced conversions of nations, and the Nazi Holocaust in which the Catholic Pope was allied with Axis forces.*

That's another fine example of Christian charity. The above paragraph consists mainly of ideas from Dave Hunt's 1994 book *A Woman Rides the Beast*. As ridiculous as it seems, it has hooked a lot of anti-Catholics who seem more interested in Catholic bashing than intelligent thought. Just recently, I read the same thing in a book by a Protestant Minister, who also identified the Pope as the Anti-Christ.

Lately, however, many are of the belief that the President of the United States or various members of

Congress are in fact the Anti-Christ, so at least Pope Benedict is off the hook for the moment.

By the way, would you like to know who the anti-Christ is? The Bible tells us, but not in the Book of Revelation. It is actually in 1 John 2:22-23.

A lot of Protestants have been taught that the harlot of Babylon in chapter 17 of the Book of Revelation is the Catholic Church. Off the subject for just a second, but does anything pop out at you here? Remember Sola Scriptura? Remember the Protestant belief that they only rely on their personal interpretation of Scripture? Remember how they claim that their beliefs come only from the Bible and not from men? So, do you think all of these Protestants came to the same conclusion by themselves, or was their interpretation in fact guided by other (fallible) humans?

So who is the Whore of Babylon? Let's skin this one and see what's inside.

The Catholic Church has not defined exactly what these passages refer to, so as a Catholic I am free to use my own interpretation as long as I stay within the overall parameters of Church teaching. Now when I do that, the Sola Scriptura Protestant must accept it because their school of thought is that every individual (including a Catholic) has the right to his/her own interpretation. The Protestant may disagree with my interpretation, but unless he is a hypocrite, he must allow that I have the same right as he does to my own interpretation. I'm not going to just leave it at my interpretation, though. I think I can show you who the Whore of Babylon is using (once again) Scripture, historical fact and common sense.

I agree with many theologians who think the Whore of Babylon is a symbol of the City of Jerusalem. I can show you that and at the same time show you that the harlot cannot be the Catholic Church. Here we go...

**Revelation 17:1** *"...I will show you the judgment on the great harlot who lives near the many waters."*

The nation of Israel is often referred to as a harlot in the Old Testament. Check this out:

**Hosea 9:1**: *"Rejoice not, O Israel! Exult not like the peoples; for you have played the harlot, forsaking your God. You have loved a harlot's hire upon all threshing floors."*

So why is Israel sometimes called a harlot in the Old Testament? Many times in Scripture, the relationship between God and Israel is spoken of as a marriage. What we see happen in several cases is that Israel would sort of cheat on God and turn to the worship of false gods. So, when Israel would forsake her true Spouse, she was called a harlot (a whore).

**Revelation 17:3:** *"...I saw a woman seated on a scarlet beast that was covered with blasphemous names, with seven heads and ten horns."*

**Revelation 17:9-10:** *"This calls for a mind with wisdom: the seven heads are seven hills on which the* *woman is seated; they are also seven kings, five of whom have fallen, one is, the other has not yet come..."*

So the seven hills refer to the beast upon which the woman sits, not the woman herself. Most Catholic and Protestant writers that I have seen agree that the beast is symbolic of Rome and the Roman Empire.

*"Well, that just proves my point. The Catholic Church 'sits' on Rome, so the Catholic Church is in fact the 'whore of Babylon'."*

Not so fast, Skippy. Let's look at verse 18:

**Revelation 17:18:** *"And the woman that you saw is the **great city** which has dominion over the kings of the earth."*

So the harlot is a "great city" which has dominion over the kings of the earth. That has to be talking about Rome and the Roman Empire, right? Well, you just saw that the *beast* that the woman is sitting on is Rome. So if the beast is Rome and the woman is also Rome, well, that just don't make no sense whatsoever. How can they both be Rome? They are clearly two separate entities in Revelation.

*"Well of course the beast is Rome, the city on seven hills, but the harlot is the city within the city: Vatican City, where the Catholic Church is headquartered."*

"Well, there's a small problem with that: That's not what the Bible says. There is no mention of Vatican City or a city within a city, so we probably shouldn't add words to the Bible, should we? Also, Vatican City did not exist until the early 20th century. It did not exist until about 1900 years after the Book of Revelation was written. So, it could not, and did not, have dominion over the kings of the earth when John wrote it. And remember, the Bible talks of the harlot in the *present tense:* ...IS the great city which HAS dominion over the kings of the earth."[31]

Next problem: the harlot is clearly identified as a city, not a Church. Is someone trying to add to the Bible here?

**Revelation 17:16:** *"And the ten horns that you saw, they and **the beast will hate the harlot**; they will make her desolate and naked, and devour her flesh, and burn her up with fire."*

So Rome will burn Vatican City? As John Martignoni said: "There goes a bunch of tourist revenue!" Now instead, what if the beast is Rome or the Roman Empire, and the harlot is Jerusalem? That would make sense. That looks like a reference to the destruction of Jerusalem. Rome sacked and burned Jerusalem in 70 A.D., leaving her naked and burned up with fire, just like the Bible says.

**Revelation 17:6:** *"And I saw the woman drunk with the blood of the saints and the blood of the martyrs of Jesus."*

---

[31] John Martignoni, Bible Christian Society, www.biblechristiansociety.com

Ok, so the woman is drunk with the blood of the saints and martyrs. Let's look at another verse where Jesus is speaking to the scribes and Pharisees:

**Matthew 23:33-38:** *"You serpents, you brood of vipers, how can you flee from the judgment of Gehenna? Therefore, behold, I send to you prophets and wise men and scribes;* **some of them you will kill and crucify, some of them you will scourge in your synagogues** *and pursue from town to town, so that there may come upon you* **all the righteous blood shed upon earth**, *from the righteous blood of Abel to the blood of Zechariah, the son of Barachiah, whom you murdered between the sanctuary and the altar.* **Amen, I say to you, all these things will come upon this generation. Jerusalem, Jerusalem, you who kill the prophets and stone those sent to you**, *how many times I yearned to gather your children together, as a hen gathers her young under her wings, but you were unwilling!* <u>**Behold, your house will be abandoned, desolate**</u>*."*

Jesus says he will send prophets and wise men and scribes to **Jerusalem**. He says they will be killed and scourged and persecuted. Does that sound to you like Jerusalem will be drunk with the blood of saints and martyrs just like the harlot?

Now go read Revelations 18:21-24 and see what happens to the "great city". Does it remind you of something abandoned and desolate, just like in the passage above where Jesus is referring to Jerusalem? Read verse 24 carefully:

**Revelations 18:24:** *"In her was found the blood of prophets and holy ones and all who have been slain on the earth."*

So if all of the blood of the prophets and holy ones and all who have been slain on earth, and the blood of those sent by Jesus who are yet to be crucified, killed, scourged and persecuted are upon Jerusalem in Matthew 23; then once again it looks to me like Jerusalem is the harlot of Babylon.

Here's something else: The harlot of Babylon is referred to as the "great city," in Revelation 17:18 and in a few verses in chapter 18. Knowing that, let's look at Rev 11:8, "*...and their dead bodies will lie in the street of the **great city** which is allegorically called Sodom and Egypt, **where their Lord was crucified**.*" So the "great city" is where their Lord was crucified... Wait, wasn't our Lord crucified in Jerusalem? So, is the "great city" Jerusalem in Rev 11, but then all of a sudden it becomes Rome in Rev 17?

Martignoni makes two more points definitely worth considering:

1) That the Jews and the Romans were both on the same side in terms of persecuting Christians for a time. Jerusalem was riding on the back of Rome in that regard. But, again, they had a falling out and the Jews rebelled against Rome...who then hated the harlot and made her desolate and naked and devoured her flesh and burned her with fire...literally.

2) Jerusalem can be said to have dominion over all the kings of the earth. In the Old Testament, Israel is referred to as the "first born" of the Lord. The first born has dominion over all

the other sons and daughters...all the other nations of the earth. So, in that sense, Jerusalem (as the capital of Israel) has dominion over the kings of the earth.

Catholic Answers did a fine job of explaining Hunt's identification of the Catholic Church as the harlot because of the color of priest garb:

"Hunt states, "She [the Whore] is clothed in 'purple and scarlet' (verse 4), the colors of the Catholic clergy." He then cites the *Catholic Encyclopedia* to show that bishops wear certain purple vestments and cardinals wear certain red vestments.

Hunt ignores the obvious symbolic meaning of the colors—purple for royalty and red for the blood of Christian martyrs. Instead, he is suddenly literal in his interpretation. He understood well enough that the woman symbolizes a city and that the fornication symbolizes something other than literal sex, but now he wants to assign the colors a literal, earthly fulfillment in a few vestments of certain Catholic clergy.

Purple and red are not the dominant colors of Catholic clerical vestments. White is. All priests wear white (including bishops and cardinals when they are saying Mass)—even the pope does so.

The purple and scarlet of the Whore are contrasted with the white of the New Jerusalem, the Bride of Christ (Rev. 19:8). This is a problem for Hunt for three reasons: (a) we have already noted that the dominant color of Catholic clerical vestments is white, which would identify them with New Jerusalem if the color is taken literally; (b) the clothing of the Bride is given a symbolic interpretation ("the righteous acts of the saints;" 19:8); implying that the clothing of the Whore should also be given a symbolic meaning; and (c) the identification of the Bride as *New* Jerusalem (Rev. 3:12, 21:2, 10) suggests that the Whore may be *old* (apostate) Jerusalem—a contrast used elsewhere in Scripture (Gal.

4:25–26).

Hunt ignores the liturgical meaning of purple and red in Catholic symbolism. Purple symbolizes repentance, and red honors the blood of Christ and the Christian martyrs.

It is appropriate for Catholic clerics to wear purple and scarlet, if for no other reason because they have been liturgical colors of the true religion since ancient Israel.

Hunt neglects to remind his readers that God commanded that scarlet yarn and wool be used in liturgical ceremonies (Lev. 14:4, 6, 49–52; Num. 19:6), and that God commanded that *the priests' vestments* be made with purple and scarlet yarn (Ex. 28:4–8, 15, 33, 39:1–8, 24, 29)."[32]

**The Pope is rich with his robe and his big hat.**

*"The Catholic Church is enormously wealthy. If they were true Christians, they could sell all of their precious gold, works of art, etc. and do so much good in the world. Supposedly priests, monks and nuns take a vow of poverty. They don't look too poor to me."*

Great idea. We could sell 1200 year old churches and monasteries, and they could be converted to say, condos. We could tear down and sell Michelangelo's *The Last Judgment* or Botticelli's *Scenes of the Life of Moses*. That would bring a pretty penny. Maybe the U.S. government could follow suit and sell the Smithsonian or Mount Rushmore. I bet Bill Gates or Donald Trump would love to have their faces carved there.

---

[32] Catholic Answers, *"Hunting the whore of Babylon"*, (San Diego: Catholic Answers, 2004)

While we are on the subject, not all of the Catholic clergy take a vow of poverty. Some are required to, but some aren't. So is the Vatican rich? Not really, in fact the Vatican typically runs a budget deficit. The following is from the C.I.A.'s World Factbook:

**Economy** - overview: This unique, noncommercial economy is supported financially by an annual contribution (known as Peter's Pence) from Roman Catholic dioceses throughout the world; by the sale of postage stamps, coins, medals, and tourist mementos; by fees for admission to museums; and by the sale of publications. Investments and real estate income also account for a sizable portion of revenue. The incomes and living standards of lay workers are comparable to those of counterparts who work in the city of Rome.

**Budge**t: revenues: $310 million
expenditures: $307 million (2006)[33]

The truth is that the Catholic Church is the largest non-governmental source of emergency aid, medical, educational, housing and food aid with billions spent annually. Also, because of the nature of the Church, the clergy and volunteers, overhead costs are generally lower than nearly any other organization on the planet.

Let me tell you about just ONE of the MANY charitable organizations that are part of the Catholic Church: the Knights of Columbus (of which I am a proud member).

---

[33] https://www.cia.gov/library/publications/the-world-factbook/print/vt.html

"As an organization the Knights have:
• Contributed to charity. In 2005 total contributions to charity were roughly $140 million dollars.
• Volunteered. Annual volunteer hours by Knights for charitable causes were over 64 million hours.
• Donated blood. 400,000 Knights donated blood during the year
• Visited the sick and bereaved. Knights made more than 5.4 million visits to the sick and bereaved
• During the past decade the Knights have donated more than $1.2 billion to charity and provided in excess of 574 million hours of volunteer service in support of charitable causes.
• Beyond financial support, the Knights of Columbus have answered the pope's call to active lay involvement in the Church as part of the New Evangelization. In addition to the countless hours and dollars the Knights of Columbus has put at the service of the Church, the organization has also stood alongside the pope on a wide range of social issues, seeking to answer the pope's call to spread the Gospel and foster a Culture of Life.
• Made the "Pledge of Allegiance" a patriotic oath and a public prayer - in 1954, Congress after a campaign by the Knights of Columbus, added the words, 'under God,' to the Pledge.
Local Councils will be involved in the following (and more):
• Supporting Seminarians and Religious
• Offering college scholarships to deserving Catholic youths
• Providing support to individuals and families in our communities
• Supporting Birthright, Special Olympics, various Catholic Charities and other Charities (I think the Knights are the largest single supporters of Birthright and the Special Olympics)
• Supporting your Parish youth group and other local Catholic causes."[34]

---

[34] http://forums.catholic.com/showthread.php?t=196433

John Allen, Jr., a Vatican correspondent for National Catholic Reporter, an independent weekly, told an audience at Marquette University that "most public conversation about the Vatican is unrealistic. It is much more driven by misperceptions ... that form a kind of mythology. Here's some of what he said:

"• The myth of Vatican wealth. "At the Vatican, everything is for sale, in the popular mind," Allen said. In reality, the Vatican's annual operating budget is about $260 million. Allen contrasted that to Harvard University, which has an annual operating budget of $1.3 billion.
" (Harvard) could run five Vaticans every year and still have pocket change left over for an endowed chair," Allen said, equating the Vatican's patrimony - all the assets it could sell - to that of a medium-sized Catholic university. Its total patrimony is $770 million. The University of Notre Dame's endowment is four and a half times greater, he said.
Allen noted that while people often assume a significant monetary value attached to the artwork the Vatican holds, it is not for sale.
" The Holy See's point of view is that the artwork is part of the patrimony of humanity," Allen said. It is listed as having a cash value of one euro."[35]

Much of the Vatican's treasures and artwork were donated over the centuries by people who entrusted their possessions to the Vatican's care. The Church can't really donate or sell that stuff, now can it? Suppose you donated a baptismal pool or lectern to your local church and the pastor sold it. That wouldn't make you too happy, now would it?

Another thing to keep in mind is that a lot of the art work is no longer owned by the Vatican, but by a

---

[35] www.catholiccitizens.org/platform/platformview.asp?c=14358

separate organization, The Vatican Museum. This museum has a similar relationship to the Vatican state as the Smithsonian does with the U.S. Government.

## Chapter Eleven
## Put the kids to bed, we need to talk...

### The Priest abuse scandal

We've all seen the headlines of horrendous reports of Priests accused of sexually abusing the young people they were ordained to serve. There is no question that those Priests' actions damaged many of these kids for the rest of their lives. I know; I grew up with some of them, and one of my Priests was an offender. Although I never personally saw him do anything inappropriate, he did so with some of my friends. This Priest was well liked by kids my age in our Parish; and we all thought he was "pretty cool".

Back in those days, this sort of crime was not talked about much. It seems it was almost too horrible to understand. Now that we know more about this type of behavior, and we know that child molesters will often take up a position through which they have access to kids, it makes a bit more sense why some wanted to shield their behavior by becoming Priests. Looking back at that Priest, I am convinced that he was a child molester first and foremost and a Priest merely out of convenience.

To add scandal to scandal, some of the Bishops involved chose to transfer these Priests instead of taking more direct action. Some of the transferred Priests re-offended and were transferred again. So you had tragic actions by some Priests against the most innocent of their flock, and in some cases you had Bishops who took actions that are impossible to explain or defend; at least I can't. (However, to their credit, at the time common thought among psychologists was that this type of behavior was curable and that there was a good chance for success with counseling. Many Bishops followed this advice.)

The Catholic Church has paid massive amounts of money to settle lawsuits, has apologized repeatedly, and has taken great steps to try to prevent this from happening again. Let's pray that they are successful.

The purpose of this chapter is not to defend the actions of these Priests and Bishops. As I said, I certainly can't. The purpose here is merely to defend the Church against some charges made by anti-Catholics who seem gleeful when a report surfaces of a sinful Catholic Priest.

Anti-Catholics attempt to use this issue to show that since some Priests perpetrated horribly sinful acts, the Catholic Church cannot be the Church established by Christ. Let's look at it in light of what happened in Scripture.

Read Luke 6:12. The night before Jesus chose his first disciple; He went up on the mountain and prayed all night. "He talked to God the Father about who He should choose to be among His twelve; the same twelve He would send out to preach the good news in His name. He gave the twelve the power to cast out demons, cure the sick, and forgive sin. These twelve watched Christ perform countless miracles and they themselves worked miracles in His name.

Despite that, one of the twelve turned out to be a traitor. Judas had seen Jesus walk on water and raise people from the dead, yet he betrayed Him. We read in Scripture that Judas allowed Satan to enter him and then handed Jesus over with a kiss."[36]

**Luke 22:48:** *"Jesus said to him, 'Judas, would you betray the Son of Man with a kiss?'"*

"Jesus didn't choose Judas to betray him. But Judas was always free, and he used his freedom to allow Satan to enter into him, and by his betrayal Jesus was crucified and executed. But God foresaw this evil and used it to accomplish the ultimate good: the redemption of the world.

The point is, sometimes God's chosen ones betray him. That is a fact that we have to confront. **If the early Christians had focused only on the scandal caused by Judas, the Church would have been finished before it even started to grow. Instead they recognized that you don't judge a movement by those who don't live it but by those who do.**

Rather than focusing on the betrayer, they focused on the other eleven on account of whose work, preaching, miracles, and love for Christ we are here today. It is on account of the other eleven-all of whom except John were martyred for Christ and for the gospel they proclaimed-that we ever heard the saving word of God, that we ever received the sacraments of eternal life.

We are confronted by the same scandalous reality today. We can focus on those who have betrayed the Lord, those who abused rather than loved the people whom they were called to serve. Or we can focus, as did the early Church, on those who have remained faithful, those priests who are still

---

[36] Fr. Robert Landry, *"A Crisis of Saints"*, Catholic Answers, 2004

offering their lives to serve Christ and you out of love. The secular media almost never focuses on the good "eleven,"

the ones whom Jesus has chosen who remain faithful, who live lives of quiet holiness. But we the Church must keep the terrible scandal that we are witnessing in its true and full perspective."[37]

I remember reading the account of a priest who was in the check-out line at a grocery store. Ahead of him was a young mother with her small child sitting in the grocery cart facing her (and the priest). The child was smiling at the priest and the priest smiled back and waved. The mother turned around, glared at the priest and blocked her child's view. I suppose she felt the priest would attack her child in the grocery store. Father Robert Landry, who wrote the above quote, had a similar experience.

So does it seem that there is a notion out there that all priests are child molesters? I don't know how that could be. It certainly can't come from our extremely fair secular media, now can it? I mean, it's not like they front page, top of the news hour report any and all scandals of the Church, now is it? (Yep, once again sarcasm rears its ugly head.)

Well, what's the truth then? Just how prevalent are abusive priests? I bet there's some statistics available…

---

[37] Fr. Robert Landry, *"A Crisis of Saints"*, Catholic Answers, 2004

**Sexual Child Abuse Rates:**

| | |
|---|---|
| Catholic Priests | .2-1.7%[38] |
| Protestant Clergy | 2-3%[39] |
| General Population | 1-5%[40] |
| School Teachers and staff | 13.5%[41] |

Here's part of a story from the Associated Press:

"INDIANAPOLIS -- Under pressure to fight child sex abuse, the Southern Baptist Convention's executive committee said Tuesday that the denomination should not create its own database to help churches identify predators or establish an office to field abuse claims.

The report decried sexual abuse as reprehensible and a sin. But the Southern Baptist principle of local church autonomy means it's up to individual churches, and not the convention, to screen employees and take action against offenders, the committee said."[42]

---

[38] Philip Jenkins, *Pedophiles and Priests* (New York: Oxford University Press), pp. 50 and 81.

[39] Ibid, pp. 50 and 81.

[40] Dr. Gene Abel, *Thieves of Childhood*, CNN Specials Transcript #454-Thieves of Childhood.

[41] Daniel Wishnietsky, "Reported and Unreported Teacher-Student Sexual Harassment," *Journal of Ed Research*, Vol. 3, 1991, pp. 164-69.

[42] Eric Gorski, *Southern Baptists reject sex-abuse database*, The Associated Press, June 10, 2008

Once again, I'm not picking on any one group, but why does it seem that this scandal is laid only at the foot of the Catholic Church? Those Protestants who wish to attack the Church based upon the priest abuse scandal would do well to visit this website: www.stopbaptistpredators.org, as well as others which shed light on similar scandals in Christian churches. If you research the statistics, you would be far more comfortable if your child is with a Catholic Priest or Protestant Minister than you would be if he or she is with a school teacher or physician. It is also far more likely for a child to be molested by a family member or the general population than members of the Christian clergy of all faiths.

**Spiritual Suicide**
*"Why should I listen to what a priest has to say? They need to worry more about molesting kids than what I do. The Church can't be true if God's so-called chosen ones can do the types of things we've been reading about!"*

Unfortunately, I hear that often, not from Protestants, but from fallen-away Catholics. Some call this spiritual suicide; abandoning the entire Church because of the actions of a few. If you fall into that category, you should reread this excerpt that was quoted above:

"If the early Christians had focused only on the scandal caused by Judas, the Church would have been finished before it even started to grow. Instead they recognized that you don't judge a movement by those who don't live it but by those who do."[43]

Let's stop and think a minute. If Jesus really established a Church (as we have shown), and He said that the gates of Hell would not prevail against this Church, does it make sense that Satan is *actually trying* to prevail against this Church? Makes sense to me! It also would seem that one way to do it would be through this very scandal. The great thing is that Jesus promised us that Satan would not be successful. The Catholic Church will not fail.

Some people are predicting that the Church is in for a rough time, and maybe it is. But the Church will survive because the Lord will make sure it survives. One of the greatest comeback lines in history was uttered two hundred years ago. As his armies were swallowing up the countries of Europe, French emperor Napoleon is reported to have said to Church officials, *"Je détruirai votre église"* ("I will destroy your Church")." When informed of the emperor's words, Ercole Cardinal Consalvi, one of the great statesmen of the papal court, replied, "He will never succeed. We have not managed to do it ourselves!" If bad popes, immoral priests, and countless sinners in the Church hadn't succeeded in destroying the Church from within, Cardinal Consalvi was saying, how did Napoleon think he was going to do it from without?

The Cardinal was pointing to a crucial truth: Christ will never allow his Church to fail. He promised that the gates of hell would not prevail against his Church (Matt. 16:18); that the barque of Peter, the Church sailing through time to its eternal port in heaven, will never capsize-not because those in the boat won't do everything sinfully possible to overturn it but because Christ, who is captain of the boat, will never

---

[43] Fr. Robert Landry, *"A Crisis of Saints"*, Catholic Answers, 2004

allow it to happen.[44]

## Contraception

*"The Catholic Church believes that contraception is sinful. I guess it's easy for some unmarried priest to say that, but let <u>him</u> try raising and paying for all of these kids."*

Poo-Yie! This is a hot topic. Non-Catholics think we're nuts and Cafeteria Catholics skip right by this one in line. I hate to admit it, but I practiced contraception myself at one time. I didn't really believe there was anything wrong with it, and I did not accept the Church's teaching. Yeah, I'm a reformed Cafeteria Catholic too...

Up until the 1930's, <u>all</u> Christian faiths agreed with Catholic teaching that contraception was an evil act and was sinful. In 1930, the Anglican Church held the Lambeth Conference and announced that contraception was allowable in *some* circumstances. Not long after that, they went the rest of the way and allowed it in all circumstances. Since then, every other Protestant denomination has followed suit. The Catholic Church is the **only** Christian Church whose teaching has not changed.

By the way, are you in favor of abortion? No one reading this book should be, but I bet many of you don't know that certain contraceptives will induce an abortion. So, if you are a big fan of "the pill" or certain

---

[44] Fr. Robert Landry, *"A Crisis of Saints"*, Catholic Answers, 2004

other contraceptives, you might ought to do a little research into what you are taking. You may have inadvertently aborted your child, rather than prevented her conception. I can only pray that is something I am not guilty of.

Ok, now that I've depressed both of us, let's get back to work. Where does the Catholic Church get this insane notion that we shouldn't practice contraception? Sit back and let me tell you about this fella named Onan.

We find Onan in the Bible in Genesis 38. Now what happened is this fella Judah married a lady named Shua and as the Bible says Judah "had relations with her". From those "relations", they had a few sons. Two of them were named Er and Onan. Er married a lady named Tamar. The Bible tells us that Er "greatly offended the Lord, so the Lord took his life".

I remember reading a news story a few years ago about a group of guys playing golf. A lightning storm broke out, and one of the golfers (I bet he was drinking) looked up to the sky, held his hands in the air and said "GOD, you (bad word). If you exist, strike me dead now!" Guess what happened. BAM! (It's never a good idea to "greatly offend the Lord"). Anyway, I bet something like that happened to Er, although I don't think he was a golfer, but you get the point.

Next, we read that Judah told his other son, Onan, to "unite with" Tamar, to preserve his brother's line. Now Onan didn't want to do that, not because Tamar was ugly or anything (at least the Bible doesn't say that), but Onan knew that the descendants "would not be counted as his". The Bible then tells us that whenever Onan had relations with Tamar, he would "spill his seed on the ground".

It seems Er, Onan and even that golfer had something in common: They didn't learn not to "greatly offend the Lord". Well, guess what happened. That's right: BAM!, and down goes Onan.

All of this seems like a really weird story to us, having to have relations with your sister-in-law after your brother dies, but that's the way things were. The point of the story is that God killed Onan because he "spilled his seed on the ground", or practiced contraception.

*"Wrong. God killed Onan because he did not fulfill his duty to have relations with Tamar, not because he spilled his seed."*

That's what they say, but get this: There was this law called the Levirate law which came from the Latin word *levir* which means "a husband's brother". You can read about the Levirate law in Deuteronomy 25, but just to make it easy, I'll type it out for you:

**Deuteronomy 25:5-6:** *"When brothers live together* (share property) *and one of them dies without a son, the widow of the deceased shall not marry anyone outside the family; but her husband's brother shall go to her and perform the duty of a brother-in-law by marrying her. The first-born son she bears shall continue the line* *of the deceased brother, that his name may not be blotted out from Israel.*

The claim that opponents of the Church's teaching on contraception make is that God was angry with Onan because he didn't fulfill the law, <u>not</u> because he "spilled his seed". If you believe that, you didn't read the rest of the passage:

**Deuteronomy 25:7-10:** *"If, however, a man does not care to marry his brother's wife, she shall go up to the elders at the gate and declare, 'My brother-in-law does not intend to perform his duty toward me and refuses to perpetuate his brother's name in Israel.' Thereupon the elders of his city shall summon him and admonish him. If he persists in saying, 'I am not willing to marry her,' his sister-in-law, in the presence of the elders, shall go up to him and strip his sandal from his foot and spit in his face, saying publicly, 'This is how one should be treated who will not build up his brother's family!' And his lineage shall be spoken of in Israel as 'the family of the man stripped of his sandal.'*

So you see that under the law, if the brother-in-law merely failed to uphold the obligation, the penalty was that he would be publicly humiliated by the sister-in-law, not killed. That means that the argument against Church teaching about contraception does not hold water. The only difference between Onan and the example in Deuteronomy is that Onan "spilled his seed on the ground". The Catholic Church calls this the sin of "Onanism".

Now for those of you who are Protestant, here are a couple of quotes you may be interested in:

"How great, therefore, the wickedness of [fallen] human nature is! How many girls there are who **prevent conception** and kill and expel tender fetuses, although procreation is the work of God! Indeed, some spouses who marry and live together...have various ends in mind, but rarely children." **Martin Luther**

"The voluntary spilling of semen outside of intercourse between man and woman is a monstrous thing. Deliberately to withdraw from coitus in order that semen may fall on the ground is doubly monstrous. For this to extinguish the hope of the [human] race and to kill before he is born the hoped-for offspring." **John Calvin**

The Church teaches that there are unitive and procreative aspects to the marital act. It unites husband and wife, but it must remain open to the possibility of procreation. The question always comes up about what exactly is or is not sinful in marital relations. It's a little hard to get an easy answer from the Catechism, so I'll see if I can't give you my understanding of it: It is ok to do almost anything to lead up to the act, as long as the man, uh, "finishes" where he is supposed to. If you need any more information than that, talk to your priest. That ain't my job.

### Uh, let's just call it "selfishness"

I remember in school once when a priest and nun came into class. The nun ushered the girls to another classroom, and the priest stayed with us guys. It was time for "the talk". No, not "THE talk", they were just there to tell us a few things that can lead developing kids to sin. I remember the priest telling us about this one sin that is committed alone and he called it a sin of "selfishness".

Now this is going to be a real short section, one, because I don't want to talk about it; and two, because I already told you why we consider it a sin. Masturbation is a sin for the same reason that Onanism is a sin. The Catechism tells us that the act is intrinsically evil, and that certain factors can lessen moral culpability, and that's all I'm gonna say about that. Go read it for yourself.

## Chapter Twelve
## Questions for Protestants

Here are a few questions that Protestants may want to think about, and Catholics may want to ask of Protestants in their discussions. Now, this isn't meant to stump someone or start an argument, they are just some things to reflect upon. For the Protestants, though, it may pay you to give these questions a lot of thought. If nothing else, they may help you learn a bit more about your own faith, and that's always a good thing. Hey, why not ask your Pastor these questions too?

### The Bible

-**Would you use as your Old Testament Scripture the same books used by Jesus, the Apostles and the early Church?**

-**Did you know that Protestant and Catholic scholars agree that the first Christians used the Septuagint, which contained the Deuterocanonical books?**

-**As Christians, do you think we should follow the Apostles and the early Church and continue to accept these seven books, or, should we use a version <u>later</u> chosen by some, but not all, Jews?**

-**Did you know that the 1611 version of the King James Bible (a Protestant Bible) contained the Deuterocanonical books, even though they were later removed from Protestant Bibles?**

-If the Deuterocanonical books were part of Scripture for the first 1500 years of Christianity, what would justify removing those same books only 500 years ago?

-If your church accepts the Deuterocanonical books (Judith, Tobit, Maccabees I&II, Wisdom, Ecclesiasticus [Sirach] and Baruch), given what is written in 2 Maccabees 12:44-46, do you now accept prayers for the dead?

-The Catholic Church chose the canon of the Bible. Was the Church inspired by the Holy Spirit when it decided which books would be included and which omitted?

-Was Martin Luther inspired by the Holy Spirit when he removed seven of those books and parts of Daniel and Esther <u>1200 years later</u>?

-If you believe in a literalist interpretation of Scripture, how do you explain John chapter 6, where we are told to actually "eat Jesus' flesh"?

-If everything we need to know as Christians is in the Bible, then where in the Bible does it tell us which books are supposed to be in the Bible?

-Since we know that there were many books around at the time which did and did not make it into the canon of the Bible, is the Table of Contents in your Bible divinely inspired?

**Where in the Bible does it say:**

**-Scripture alone is the sole rule of faith for Christians?**
**-We are saved or justified by faith alone?**
**-Baptism is a symbolic gesture that the already saved believer makes to show his commitment to God?**
**-That every individual, Christian or not, has the right to interpret every single passage of Scripture on their own in order to determine, by their own authority, what is true doctrine and what is false doctrine?**
**-That you are to have altar calls?**
**-That you are to meet at your church every Wednesday night?**
**-Or, that you are to go to church on Sunday?**
**-That it is ok to disagree on the "non-essential" doctrines as long as you agree on the "essential" doctrines?**
**-That there is even such a thing as a "non-essential" doctrine, a non-essential part of the Word of God?**
Hint: None of those things are in Scripture.

**-I bet you love Scripture. Would you feel cheated if there were more books in the Bible than you had been told?**
**-Did the first-century Christians bring their Bible with them to Church?**
If you answer no, and you have to because there was no Bible, then you must admit that "Sola Scriptura", or the "Bible alone" teaching does not go back to early Christianity. It wasn't started by Jesus or the Apostles, and it wasn't practiced by early Christians.

## Salvation

- If you believe in "Once Saved, Always Saved", how can someone who is already saved be found to be unworthy of receiving the Lord's Supper? (I Cor. 11:27)

-If we are saved by faith alone, do we need to love one another or do we even need to love God to be saved?

-If you have faith, but have not works, can your faith save you? (James 2:14-17)

-If salvation by faith alone is the most central and most important Christian doctrine, then why does the phrase "faith alone" appear only once in all of Scripture, and that is to say that we are not justified by "faith alone"? (James 2:24)

-Is whether or not we have faith God's sole criteria for judging us worthy of salvation? (Matthew 24:14-30 & 31-46, John 15:1-6, Romans 2:6, Revelation 20:13) **Why don't they say we will be judged by our faith?**

-Christ redeemed all men with His death on the cross. In other words, He paid the price for all men's sins. Yet, not all men are saved. What is the difference between those who are merely redeemed and the subset of that group who are redeemed and saved? Is that something that Jesus did, or is it something each saved individual did?

If it is something that the individual did, isn't that a "work"?

**-Do we have to forgive others in order to have our sins forgiven by God?**

## The Church

**-Is your church autonomous? In other words, is there a hierarchy in your church, or is it governed locally? Does your local church answer to a larger body?**

**-If your church is autonomous, how do you compare that to the "churches" we read about in the New Testament? Didn't those churches fall under a central authority? Don't Peter and Paul's letters to these churches signify that they were under a central leadership?**

**- Does your church give you guidance on what conditions make you "unworthy" to receive the Lord's Supper?**
In Scripture we are told that one who eats the flesh or drinks the blood of the Lord unworthily will have to answer for the body and blood of the Lord. Paul here was speaking to baptized Christians, so it cannot mean that just anyone who is baptized or "saved" can receive the Lord's Supper.

**-Throughout Scripture we are told about "prayer and fasting". Does your church follow the practice of fasting?**

-When a member of your church is sick, do the presbyters of the church pray over him and anoint him with oil in the name of the Lord as Scripture directs us? (James 5:14)

-If your Pastor began teaching things that the church membership felt were contrary to Scripture, could your church (or church board) vote to have that Pastor removed?

-Would that vote, which would concern a matter of faith or morals, be guided by the Holy Spirit? In other words, is there some guarantee that the congregation would be correct and the Pastor wrong?

-Where in Scripture do you find the practice of a church congregation deciding matters of faith and morals?

-Where in Scripture does it say that a church membership may remove a church leader by popular vote?

-For a Christian, what is the pillar and foundation of truth? Is it the Bible? (1 Timothy 3:15)

-Would you consider your church to be the "pillar and foundation" of truth as described in the Bible?

-Where does it say in the Bible that God's revelation to men ended with the death of the last Apostle?

-If you feel that God's revelation did in fact end with the death of the last Apostle, isn't that a non-Biblical tradition?

-Where in Scripture is the concept of an "invisible church" mentioned?

-As Christians, we share a significant bond, but when Jesus spoke of His church, do you think this "invisible connection" is all that He had in mind?

-Would you have been considered a member of Christ's Church if you had followed different teachings and leaders not approved by the Apostles, even though you professed belief in Christ?

-If God alone can forgive sins, and we are to confess our sins only to God, and not to men, then why does Matthew say that God gave the authority on earth to forgive sins to "men" (plural)? (Matthew 9:6-8)

-And why does Scripture tell us to confess our sins to one another? (James 5:16)

-And why does Jesus give His disciples the power to forgive or retain sins in the first place? (John 20:23)

**-What is your church's <u>official</u> teaching on the following:**

**Contraception?**
And if your church does not prohibit contraception, why did it change its teaching on a matter of faith or morals?

**Embryonic Stem Cell Research?**

**Euthanasia?**

**Human Cloning?**

**Divorce and Remarriage?**

**Same sex marriage?**

**Abortion?**

**Does your church even <u>have</u> an official, documented and universal teaching on these subjects?**

**If so, does that teaching apply to <u>all</u> churches within your denomination, or just to your local church?**

**If so, is that teaching <u>binding</u> on all people in your denomination?**

**Would you say that you consider the early Church to be the model of authentic Christian belief and practice?**

-Were those first Christians true Christians even though they didn't rely on the Bible alone as their source of truth?

-Does the Bible say that there would come a time when we should no longer follow the teaching of the apostles handed on in the Church and look only to written Scripture?

- Or, does it support the validity of the apostolic teaching?

-Is the Holy Spirit able to preserve the oral teaching of the apostles as He has the written word? And if He has, would you want to know it?

-What if I were to tell you that the Holy Spirit has preserved the apostolic teaching in full—oral and written? Would it be worth the effort to investigate and find out? What if, as we see in the New Testament, God has given us more than the Bible alone as a means to know the truth? Would you accept it?

- If you don't believe the Holy Spirit infallibly guides the Catholic Church, how can you believe the Bible is the word of God? The Catholic Church declared which early writings were Scripture and which were not. Without the Catholic Church there would be no Bible.

-If Sola Fide and Sola Scriptura are the two pillars of Protestantism, why doesn't either of those terms appear in the Bible?

**-Why don't either of those *ideas* even appear in the Bible, except to show that they are both wrong?** (James 2:24 and 2 Peter 1:20)

If you have read these questions and this book with an open mind, and really contemplated them, I bet you probably have a different understanding of the Catholic Church than you previously did. If so, you probably have many more questions than you ever did about Catholicism. If you have begun to get the idea that the Catholic Church has what we call "the fullness of the faith", and what is referred to as "*More*, not just *Mere* Christianity", then maybe you owe it to yourself to look a little deeper. There's a lot at stake here.

If you are getting a bit curious, there is a great program on the Eternal Word Television Network (yeah, we have our own television network, we call it EWTN) called "The Journey Home". It is hosted by Marcus Grodi. Here's some of Marcus' story in his own words:

"My wife Marilyn and I were both lifelong Protestants, and I was an ordained Presbyterian minister, before we were received into the Catholic Church in 1992. Our journey into the Catholic Church was very exciting and fulfilling but also very lonely, because we knew only a few other ministers who had converted, we knew very few Catholics, and because none of our Protestant friends could understand why we were doing such a "foolish" thing.

After we converted, we began to meet other clergy converts as well as clergy and their families who were still on the journey home. Together we saw the need for a fellowship of converts and their families to provide a network of help to others still on the journey. This is how the *Coming Home Network International* began in 1993.

During the last 15 years, the CHNetwork has grown considerably, primarily because the Holy Spirit continues to open the hearts and minds of our separated brethren to the truth of the Catholic Faith. Every week we hear from 2-5 new Protestant ministers somewhere along their journey home. **Over these past fifteen years, we have assisted nearly 1600 ministers from over 100 non-Catholic traditions.** We have also assisted many laymen, and do this in partnership with over 10,000 life-long Catholics and converts who support our work through their prayers, fellowship, evangelistic outreach, and financial support."[45]

Can you imagine? There are enough Protestant **Ministers** converting to Catholicism that Marcus is able to fill a weekly television series. Here's his website: www.chnetwork.org

Catholic Answers has a handy webpage you may wish to visit if you are considering becoming Catholic:

http://www.catholic.com/library/How_to_Become_a_Catholic.asp

I would also recommend that you visit the forums at Catholic.com and join in the fray! The apologetics section is a great place to start, and here you will find people of all faiths (and no faith) discussing apologetics.

If you are more of a book type, I would like to recommend that you read Rome Sweet Home, by Scott Hahn. Scott is a former Protestant Minister with a

---

[45] http://www.chnetwork.org/Marcus%20Grodi%20page.html

doctorate in Theology who converted to Catholicism after asking himself, his professors, and fellow Pastors many of the same questions you saw above. He could never get an answer until he looked into the one Church that he hated: the Catholic Church. Suddenly, his questions were answered and everything made sense.

Still not convinced?

Please read this short story, courtesy of

catholicrevelations.org:

## Finding the True Church of Christ Today

The first thing to say is that you have a 1 /40,000 chance of selecting the right Christian Church at random as there are that many new ones and the list is growing all the time as new divisions are created. Consider this touching short story about a young man's journey back to the true Church of Christ and then you decide for yourself!

*One day I was pondering the question of how to find the true Church of Christ in this crazy world. All of a sudden I heard the beautiful voice of a wise man in my heart say "Seek and ye shall find!" Intrigued, I enquired further "Tell me how can I find the true Church of Christ among so many?" The voice paused for a moment. Then I heard him reply reassuringly "I could tell you myself my child but I won't. You will tell me" he said confidently. I could almost detect a twinkle in his eye as if he were stood before me. "How can that be?" I asked. The voice went on, "Have you ever heard of the 7 marks of the Church of Christ?" "I haven't." I said curiously. "They are all in the bible," He said. "If you read the bible with spiritual eyes you will be able to recognize the Church Jesus Christ founded 2000 years ago" "Where should I start?" I asked. "With the first mark, of course" he replied. "What is the first mark?" I asked.*

**"Where Peter is, there is the Church"** he replied warmly. "Where does it say that in the bible?" I asked. "Matthew 16:18" He replied. "Jesus said to St. Peter "Thou art Peter; and upon this rock I will build my church, and the gates of Hell shall not prevail against it. And I will give to thee the keys of the kingdom of heaven; and whatsoever thou shalt bind upon earth, it shall be bound also in heaven: and whatsoever thou shalt loose on earth, it shall be loosed also in heaven". "Oh" I said sceptically. He then asked me "Where today will you find the pope, the successor to St Peter? In the Lutheran, Anglican, Presbyterian, Episcopalian, Methodist, Mormon, Baptist, Pentecostal, Catholic Church? I hesitated. "The Catholic Church, I guess...but, but..." He stopped me and smiled. "Don't worry, my child, all will become clear...Do you know what the second mark of the true Church is?" "No" I said begrudgingly...

**"Where there are bishops under the pope, there is the Church."** He replied. "turn to Acts 20:28 in your bible and you will find it there" he said kindly. I looked and he was right. There it was in the good book: "the Holy Ghost has placed you bishops to rule to the Church of God, which he hath purchased with His own blood" I read and I was amazed. I always thought that the pastor ran the Church. I had never come across the word bishop before in any of the modern bibles. Then I heard him say to me again "In which Church today will you find bishops under the pope - the Lutheran, Anglican, Presbyterian, Episcopalian, Methodist, Mormon, Baptist, Pentecostal or Catholic Church? I reluctantly replied "Well it would have to be The Catholic Church but that doesn't mean...." Again the voice softly interrupted. "Be at peace my child. Would you like to know the third mark of the Church?" he asked sweetly. "Yes" I replied interestedly.

**"Where there are local priests under a bishop, there is the Church"** he replied. Now I could only ever recall elders being mentioned in the bible but not priests. I remembered that priests were required to offer sacrifices for sin in the Old Testament but didn't Jesus Christ put an end to all of this as

*High priest on the cross? But before I could say anything the voice gently invited me to read St Paul's letter to Titus 1:5 which records the apostle as stating "You shouldest ordain priests in every city" and in his letter to Timothy 1 Timothy 4:14 which says this must be done "by the imposition of the hands of the priesthood". It dawned on me that most of the churches I knew about had big ministries, even TV and radio shows, with laying on of hands, speaking in tongues and prophesy but they did not have a priesthood which could be found in every city of the world. Just at that point the voice sounded again in my heart "My child, in which Church today will you find priests in every city, under a bishop, under the pope - the Lutheran, Anglican, Presbyterian….?" "The Catholic Church of course" I interrupted sharply. By now the thought of Catholic priests and all the scandals I had heard about was making me restless but the voice intuitively asked me "Do you want to go on?" Dismissing my discouragement I replied bravely "Yes, I do". "Then pray, tell me, my son" the voice said "Do you know the 4$^{th}$ mark of the Church?" "No" I answered.*

**"Where you can confess your sins to a priest of God, there is the Church"** *he replied. For a moment the words sat calmly in my heart. But then I felt some resistance and then resentment grow in me. I lost my patience and burst out into protest. "But, but, the bible says we have only one mediator between God and man Christ Jesus!" The voice replied calmly "Have good courage my child and turn with me to the Gospel of St John 20:22-23 - Behold there what is written of Jesus' words to His chosen ones "Whose sins you shall forgive, they are forgiven them, and whose sins you shall retain, they are retained" I had never read this passage before and its words rendered me speechless. Suddenly I felt a knot loosed in my heart. I felt His voice warm me from within. There was a peaceful pause where I felt His hand take mine. Then the voice softly sounded in my heart again "Tell me, my child, which of these Churches has shepherds who can forgive you all your sins in the name of the Holy one who sent them- the Lutheran, Anglican, Presbyterian….or the Catholic?" "The Catholic…" I replied irritatingly "It would have to be the Catholic Church" Then He said to me "Be at* peace my child for the fifth mark will be of great comfort to you. Would you like to hear of it ?" "Yes" I replied, wiping the tears away from my eyes.

**"Where the bread and wine is changed into body and blood of Christ on the altar, there is the Church"** I heard the voice say. I stopped and thought about this for a minute before asking "But wasn't the bread and wine supposed to be just a symbol of Christ giving up His body and blood up for us on the cross? I asked him. "Turn to the Gospel of St John 6:51 to hear the Lord's own loving explanation" said the voice kindly: "I am the bread that came down from heaven, and the bread I will give is my flesh for the life of the world...Except you eat the flesh of the Son of man, and drink his blood, you shall not have life in you. He that eateth my flesh, and drinketh my blood, hath everlasting life: and I will raise him up in the last day. For my flesh is meat indeed: and my blood is drink indeed" Suddenly my eyes were opened and I recalled that after Jesus had said these words to his followers many of them walked away because they knew He meant them to take it literally. After all he didn't call them back to explain He was only speaking symbolically. Did Christ not prove He could change one thing into another when he transformed the water into wine at the wedding feast of Cana? And what about the multiplication of loaves and fishes He used to feed the multitude? Could he not distribute His own body in the form of bread? The voice then repeated its loving challenge "My child, in which Church can you fulfil Jesus' commandment to eat the flesh and drink the blood of the Son of Man today - the Lutheran, Anglican, Presbyterian, Episcopalian, Methodist, Mormon, Baptist, Pentecostal, Catholic Church?" This time I let him finish his list; for some reason it made my answer stand out all the more. "It is the Catholic Church!" I replied affirmatively, almost triumphantly, before clearing my throat and composing myself. "Are you now ready to hear about the $6^{th}$ mark of the Church" he said. "I am" I replied expectantly.

**"Where Christians shall call the Virgin Mother of Christ blessed, there is the Church"** I heard him announce lovingly. "Do you mean Mary?" I asked. "But wasn't she just *a woman like any other, a vessel for the birth of the saviour - surely it would be wrong to idolize a mere woman?" The voice sounded again in my heart but this time so tenderly that I got a lump in my throat. "Walk with me my son to one of my favourite places in scripture the Gospel of St <u>Luke 1:48</u> and there you will find God's handmaiden announce a prophecy about Gods faithful ones: "For behold, all generations shall call me blessed, because He that is mighty has done great things to me!" He continued "And where, in what Church of Christians today will you find them who have honoured the mother of Christ as blessed for generations – Could it be the Lutheran, Anglican, Presbyterian....?" Before he could finish I trumpeted gleefully "But everyone knows it's the Catholics who love Mary, right? "You have said it, my son" I heard him whisper. By now I found myself excited and impatient for the next instalment. "Pray tell me, dear guide, of the 7$^{th}$ mark!" I cried.*

***"Where the saints offer the incense of our prayers to God, there is the Church"*** *I heard him say affectionately. "But isn't praying to men a form of idolatry?" I asked earnestly. His sweet voice sounded again like music in my soul "Turn to the last book in your bible, my son, the book of the <u>Apocalypse 8:3</u> for the answer you seek: "And another angel came and stood before the altar having a golden censer; and there was given to him much incense that he should offer of the prayers of all saints upon the golden altar, which is before the throne of God" The scales sort of fell away from my eyes at this point and I understood that just as we can pray for one another here on earth, how powerful the prayers of the friends of God in heaven must be in our regard if we only ask for them. Then the voice in my heart returned "Where, my child, will you find a Church which asks for the prayers of the friends of God – the Lutheran, Anglican, Presbyterian… or the Catholic?" I didn't hesitate "The Catholic Church, my Lord" I said. "You have spoken the truth, my child" said the voice lovingly. "Do any doubts remain in your heart?"*

*"But what of the other 39,000 Churches that don't bear the seven marks?" I asked quizzically. He replied "turn with me*

*to St Paul's letter to the Ephesians 4:5 and hear what the apostle cries out to all doubters – there is but "one Lord, one faith and one baptism" I felt my stomach drop. I wondered how today's people could possibly recognize there is but one true faith among so many competing churches. "It was all foretold in the scriptures" the voice interrupted gently "Turn with me to hear the prophecy of the first pope about what would happen to his Church 2 Peter 2:1 "There shall be among you lying teachers, who shall bring in sects of perdition" Sects? Aren't they like splinter groups or breakaways? I thought to myself. Then the number 40,000 flashed before my mind's eye. I felt discouraged. It occurred to me, that there must be many good and sincere people in these other communities who really love Jesus and don't know any better. "But they have less spiritual food to eat because they don't have the seven marks of the true faith!" I complained. "After all they do not have a loving pope to settle disputes wisely, they don't have real bishops to serve the Churches like the apostles, they don't have priests to shepherd the lambs, or the body and blood of Christ with which to feed them, nor can they forgive sins in the name of the one who sent them, and they are often hostile about honouring the Mother of Christ and the saints?" The voice gently chimed again in my heart "Have faith, my child, and walk with me to the Gospel of John 10:16 and hear what the good Lord Jesus says - "And other sheep I have, that are not of this fold: them also I must bring, and they shall hear my voice, and there shall be one fold and one shepherd." "But who will bring them back into the fold?" I cried anxiously. Then I felt His beautiful words in the precincts of my heart again. "Turn with me to the apostle's letter to the Romans 10:13 and hear his mighty words "For whosoever shall call upon the name of the Lord, shall be saved. How then shall they call on him, in whom they have not believed? Or how shall they believe him, of whom they have not heard? And how shall they hear, without a preacher? And how shall they preach unless they be sent." The voice continued "Behold I am sending you to preach the Gospel to the poor" he thundered in my heart. "Write what you have heard" Then*

*His voice faded leaving behind it a fiery glow in my heart for those other sheep……"*[46]

Now that we got all of that out of the way, I want to thank you for taking the time to read this book. I hope I didn't offend any of you, because that was never my intention. It is a plain fact that when we defend our faith, sometimes we just have to show others where we think they are in error. Whenever I did that, I want you to know that it was not intended as an attack. As I said in the beginning of this book, my intentions are only to teach Catholics more about their faith, to teach them how to defend their faith, and to maybe teach Protestants what Catholics *really* believe. I hope I have accomplished some of that.

Hey, since you are still here, let's have a little fun. Read one more chapter for me, and I'll be done. I call this one "Catlick Fax". If you don't know what that means, it's not because you aren't Catholic, it's because you aren't Cajun; because that's just about how we would pronounce that title. Anyway, let's look at some cool things about the Catholic Church that many people don't know.

---

[46] www.catholicrevelations.org

# Chapter Thirteen
# Catlick Fax

You may be surprised to learn just how much the Catholic Church has influenced your life and the lives of folks for the past two thousand years. Here's just a few of those:

**Church on Sunday-** The Catholic Church changed the Lord's Day from the Saturday Sabbath to Sunday in honor of Christ's resurrection.

**The Calendar-** The calendar that we all use now was devised by Pope St. Gregory. It is called the Gregorian Calendar.

**The Lord's Prayer-** In Catholic Bibles, the Lord's Prayer in Matthew 6:13 does not have what is called the doxology: *"For the kingdom, the power and the glory are yours..."*; but some Protestant Bibles do contain that text. The reason Catholic Bibles do not contain that text is that the doxology is not part of Scripture and was not in the original text. Catholic monks, when copying the Bible, sometimes made notes in the margins and would often do so in red ink to make it clear that this was not Scriptural text. Apparently Protestant translators did not know that, and included the doxology as part of the Lord's Prayer, even though it was not something that Jesus said in that passage. If you have a Protestant Bible with the doxology in Matthew 6:13, compare that verse with Luke 11:2 which has the Lord's Prayer...*without the doxology!*

**Christmas and Easter-** The word "Christmas" comes from "Christ's Mass". The decision to have Christmas fall on December 25$^{th}$ was made by the Catholic Church. The Church also set the dates of observance for Easter Sunday.

**April Fool's Day-** Prior to the Gregorian Calendar, much of Europe celebrated March 25$^{th}$, the date of the Feast of the Annunciation, as the beginning of the new year. The celebration of this feast ended on April 1$^{st}$ and was celebrated with dancing and parties much like today. In 1582, Pope Gregory XIII introduced the Gregorian Calendar and New Years Day was moved to January 1$^{st}$. There were some folks who didn't know about the date change, and they continued to celebrate the New Year on April 1$^{st}$. These people were called "April Fools" and often had tricks played on them.

**<u>St. Patrick</u>-** St. Patrick was the second bishop of Ireland. Pope Celestine I entrusted St. Patrick with the mission of gathering the Irish race into the one fold of Christ. Using the single stem and triple leaf of a shamrock as an example, St. Patrick demonstrated the concept of the Holy Trinity.

**Santa Clause**- The legend of Santa Claus is based on St. Nicholas. He was the bishop of Myra in Asia Minor in the 4$^{th}$ century, and had a habit of secret gift-giving.

**The Vulgate Bible-** St. Jerome translated the Bible from Hebrew and Greek into Latin in the early 5$^{th}$ century. This early translation is called the Vulgate, because it was written in "Vulgar Latin", or everyday Latin.

**The First American Missionary-** Christopher Columbus, who sailed to America in 1492, was a Catholic. Columbus' goal was to bring the Catholic faith to the New World. In a letter he wrote to the king and queen of Spain in the 1490s, Columbus made recommendations for newly-discovered islands, including: "That there shall be a church, and parish priests or friars to administer the sacraments, to perform divine worship, and for the conversion of the Indians." Now you know why we have a group called the Knights of Columbus!

**Mardi Gras-** This holiday always falls on the Tuesday before Ash Wednesday. This holiday marks the day before the forty day period of fasting before Easter (Lent). In 325 A.D., the Council of Nicaea established a forty day Lenten season.

**Crozier-** The lacrosse crozier was so named by the first Europeans to see the sport. They thought the stick resembled a bishop's crozier- *la crosse,* in French.

**Stained Glass-** Since the majority of early Christians could not read, the Church began using stained glass windows which portrayed different scenes from Scripture. The faithful could look at these images and learn about the life of Jesus!

**The Hail Mary Pass...** "Roger Staubach, former Dallas Cowboy quarterback and member of the Pro Football Hall of Fame, allowed his Catholic faith to influence how he played. His most famous career moment was the *"Hail Mary Pass"* he threw in the 1975 playoff game against the Minnesota Vikings. With only seconds left and Dallas trailing 14-10, Staubach launched a 50-yard pass to Drew Pearson, who amazingly caught it and took the Cowboys to victory. After the game, Staubach confidently told reporters that he had prayed a *"Hail Mary"* prayer before throwing the pass, which indicated that he attributed the success of the "miraculous" play to the Virgin Mary. The term is now part of football vocabulary for passes made in desperation with very small chances of success."[47]

Here are some interesting facts about food:

**No meat on Friday-** "This tradition goes back to the first century, when Christians abstained from eating meat on Fridays to honor Jesus' death on the cross on Good Friday. Because Jesus sacrificed his flesh for the salvation of humankind, the flesh of warm-blooded animals wasn't consumed on Fridays."[48] It had absolutely nothing to do with supporting the fishing industry, as some claim.

**Coffee ...** "Probably the only food discovered by a monk and officially approved by a pope. According to legend, coffee was discovered more than a thousand years ago when a friar in an Arabian convent noticed his goats prancing on their hind legs after eating berries from a wild coffee plant. He tried the beans himself; soon afterwards a new medicine was born.

---

[47] Kelly Bowring, *"The Secrets, Chastisement and Triumph of the Two Hearts of Jesus and Mary"*, Two Hearts Press, 2009

[48] http://www.livingourfaith.net/CatholicTriviaQuestion/CatholicTr18.htm

Drinking coffee for the sheer pleasure of it didn't come until years later ... and it didn't come without a fight. Sold in popular coffeehouses known as "penny universities" and "seminars of sedition," coffee was denounced by devout Christians as "the devil's brew" and outlawed by secular authorities who saw it as an intoxicating beverage that led to "discussions of rebellion and slander of those in power." Church opposition finally ended in 1594 when Pope Clement VIII tried a cup and liked it so much that he baptized it. "We will not let coffee remain the property of Satan," he announced. "As Christians, our power is greater than Satan's; we shall make coffee our own." (Thank God!)"[49]

**Pretzels ...** "Salted breads have been around for thousands of years - but it wasn't until about 610 A.D. that an Italian monk twisted them into their distinctive crisscross shape, which is supposed to look like two arms folded in prayer. The monk created these *pretioles*, or "little gifts" to give as a reward to children who memorized their prayers. By 1200 A.D. they were popular all over Europe."[50]

**McDonald's Filet-O-Fish Sandwich ...** "Remember meatless Fridays? They were the inspiration for McDonald's Filet-O-Fish sandwich, which was developed in 1962 by Louis Groen, owner of the burger chain's franchises in Cincinnati, Ohio. His restaurants made money every day except Friday when the city's huge Catholic population skipped McDonald's in favor

---

[49] http://www.st-ignatius-loyola.com/triva_cuisine.html
[50] Ibid.

of competitors offering fish and other nonmeat entrees."[51]

**Hot Cross Buns ...** "First baked by the pagan Saxons, who called them *bouns* (Saxon for "sacred ox" - and an ancestor of the word "bun") and baked them with X marks representing ox horns. The rolls were so popular that when the Christians began converting the Saxons to Christianity, rather than abolish the rolls they just rotated them forty-five degrees, reinterpreted the pagan X mark as a Christian cross ... and passed them out during Mass to win converts."[52]

**Champagne ...** "Invented by accident when Dom Perignon, a 17th century Benedictine monk from the Champagne region of France, began stuffing corks into the bottles of wine produced at his abbey. Unlike traditional cloth rag stoppers, which allowed carbon dioxide to escape, corks were airtight and caused bubbles to form. Amazingly, Dom Perignon thought the bubbles were a sign of poor quality - and devoted his entire life to *removing* them; but he never succeeded. Louis XIV took such a liking to champagne that he began drinking it exclusively; thanks to his patronage, by the 1700s champagne was a staple of French cuisine."[53]

A lot of words we use have Catholic origins:

---

[51] http://www.st-ignatius-loyola.com/triva_cuisine.html
[52] Ibid.
[53] Ibid.

**Chapel-** "Background: When Saint Martin of Tours died in the fourth century, his admirers kept his cape - called a *capella* in Latin - and built a shrine for it. The French named the shrine the *chapelle*, and when the English borrowed the word, they dropped the "le" and applied the word to any small place of worship ... whether or not it had a cape in it.

Note: The person assigned to guard Saint Martin's cape was known as the *capellanus* ... which is the direct precursor of the English word "chaplain.""[54]

**Bonfire-** "Background: A gruesome throwback to the reign of England's King Henry VIII, who had large fires specially built and lit to burn Catholics who refused to renounce the pope and accept him as the leader of the English church. Originally spelled *bonefire*, the word gets its name from the fact that surviving Catholics plucked the bones of the dearly departed out of the ashes and preserved them as relics."[55]

**Decimate-** "Today 'decimate' means to destroy or kill a large part of something, but in the old days it was much more precise: It meant to kill every tenth person ... and has the same root as "decimal" and "December." Background: Decimation was the means by which the Roman military dealt with mutinous troops: It literally held a death lottery in which it killed one tenth of the rebellious soldiers by selecting names at random. One famous example was that of Saint Maurice and six hundred of his troops in approximately 287 A.D. When

---

[54] http://www.st-ignatius-loyola.com/triva_word-origins.html
[55] Ibid.

they refused to make sacrifices to pagan gods, one tenth of the soldiers were slaughtered. But they still refused to sacrifice, so another tenth were killed, and so on until everyone was dead - with Saint Maurice being the very last person martyred."[56]

**Cemetery-** Background: "The word comes from *koimeterion*, the Greek word for "sleeping place." The early Christians were the first people to call graveyards cemeteries - they believed the bodies of the dead would be reunited with their souls on Judgment Day, which meant the corpse's placement in the cemetery was only temporary."[57]

**Catacomb-** Background: "Yet another Catholic death innovation. The name came about by coincidence, thanks to the location of one of the early Christian grave sites on the Via Appia outside of Rome: It was *kata kumbas* - "near the low place" - between two hills."[58]

**Beg-** "In the twelfth century Lambert de Begue, an Italian cleric, founded an order of *mendicant* monks (friars who lived entirely on donations they solicited from the public). His name - pronounced *beg* - eventually became synonymous with the way his followers made their living."[59]

**Pants-** "Saint Pantaleone was a Christian physician who was beheaded in the fourth century during the

---

[56] http://www.st-ignatius-loyola.com/triva_word-origins.html
[57] Ibid.
[58] Ibid.
[59] Ibid.

reign of the Roman emperor Diocletian. His name is strikingly similar to the battle cry of the city of Venice, *Piante Lione!* ("Plant the Lion!"), so much so that Venetians made him a patron saint ... and often painted him wearing the flared trousers that were popular in the city. By the eighteenth century the garment was so closely associated with him that they were known as *pantaleones*, a term that Americans abbreviated to "pants.""[60]

**Lobby-** "In the Middle Ages when monks were the only educated people in many towns, illiterate peasants depended on them for help with letter writing, legal aid, and other services. Many monasteries built vine-covered walkways (called *lobias* in German) to accommodate the people waiting for assistance. The word lobia was adopted into the English language as the word "lobby," which eventually came to mean any public waiting area."[61]

**Dumbbells-** "Church bells were an important part of life during the Middle Ages, and ringing them properly required a surprising amount of skill. But it was almost impossible for beginners to practice without driving townspeople crazy from the noise ... at least until someone invented a set of *dumb* bells - weights suspended from ropes - that worked just like the real bells, except that they didn't make any noise. Working with the heavy weights developed the user's bell-ringing skills and his physique, so much so that non-bellringers began using them to get into shape. The

---

[60] http://www.st-ignatius-loyola.com/triva_more-word-origins.html
[61] Ibid.

name "dumbbell" came to apply to any set of weights that helped you get in shape ... whether or not they had anything to do with bells."[62]

**Garden-** "The Romans introduced horticulture to England in the first century A.D. - but when they abandoned the island in the fifth century, gardening died out except among monasteries and other religious institutions, whose gardens and orchards were often surrounded by walls or fences to *guard* against cattle and wild animals. These protected spaces became known as *guardins*, a name that eventually came to describe any planted plot of land ... whether or not it was guarded."[63]

**Raising Cain-** "The eighteenth century was an age in which children were supposed to be seen and not heard. Parents who raised rowdy, undisciplined children were said to be *raising Cains*: children who would grow up to be like the biblical Cain (who murdered his brother Abel and then denied responsibility when questioned by God). Over time, "raising cain" came to refer to the *act* of unruliness, not the child-rearing itself."[64]

**X** (The kiss symbol)- "In the Middle Ages, illiterate peasants who couldn't sign their names on important documents wrote an *X* instead - the mark of Saint Andrew. On *really* important documents the peasant had to kiss the *X* as a further sign of his sincerity. By the twentieth century the *X* and its kiss were completely

---

[62] http://www.st-ignatius-loyola.com/triva_more-word-origins.html
[63] Ibid.
[64] Ibid.

synonymous."[65] And now you know where "sealed with a kiss" comes from.

Ever wonder why some Cajun names have an "X" at the end, and some don't, and why similar French names don't? Supposedly for sort of the same reason. Illiterate Cajuns would often go to their parish priest for help on legal or other matters. When a document had to be executed, the priest would write in the person's name: James Thibodeau, and the person would make his mark at the end (his "x"). Supposedly people took this to mean that their name ended in an x. Mine does, so what does that say about my lineage...

-The Pope does not receive a salary. When Pope John Paul II died, he didn't leave any property behind except for things he used daily, and his will said that these items should be "distributed as will seem opportune".

-When a Pope needs to be elected, the Cardinals meet in a *conclave* which means a private lockable room. The Cardinals are actually locked in until they reach a decision.

How do you become a saint?
-You have to have lived a holy life,
-You have to have been dead more than five years,
-There must be at least two miracles attributed to you after you died.
If your miracles involved a cure, it must have been instantaneous and complete. There was a candidate for

---

[65] http://www.st-ignatius-loyola.com/triva_more_word_origins.html

sainthood who was rejected because the blind man he cured only had 90% sight restored.

-Every day (except for one), all over the world, the Catholic Mass is celebrated. In each Latin Rite Catholic Church, no matter where you go, the Scripture readings are the same for that day.

**Good Friday-** is the only day that no Catholic Mass is celebrated.

-It is estimated that a Catholic Mass begins every two minutes somewhere in the world.

**One Nation, Under God...** The Knights of Columbus was responsible for the addition of the words "Under God" to the Pledge of Allegiance:

"On August 21, 1952, the Supreme Council of the Knights of Columbus, at its annual meeting, adopted a resolution urging that the change be made general and copies of this resolution were sent to the President, the Vice President (as Presiding Officer of the Senate) and the Speaker of the House of Representatives. The National Fraternal Congress meeting in Boston on September 24, 1952, adopted a similar resolution upon the recommendation of its President, Supreme Knight Luke E. Hart. Several State Fraternal Congresses acted likewise almost immediately thereafter.

At its annual meeting the following year, on August 20, 1953, the Supreme Council of the Knights of Columbus repeated its resolution to make this amendment to the Pledge of Allegiance to the Flag general and to send copies of this resolve to the President, Vice President, Speaker of the House, and to each member of both Houses of Congress. From this latter action, many favorable replies were received, and a total of seventeen resolutions were

introduced in the House of Representatives to so amend the Pledge of Allegiance as set forth in the Public Law relating to the use of the flag. The resolution introduced by Congressman Louis C. Rabaut of Michigan was adopted by both Houses of Congress, and it was signed by President Eisenhower on Flag Day,
June 14, 1954, thereby making official the amendment conceived, sponsored, and put into practice by the Knights of Columbus more than three years before."[66]

**No Catholic School for you-** In 1922, the voters of Oregon passed an initiative to eliminate parochial schools (the Compulsory Education Act). This act made public schools mandatory for all children. The Society of Sisters sued Oregon Governor Walter Pierce in a case called *Pierce v. Society of Sisters.* The Supreme Court declared the law unconstitutional, and Associate Justice James Clark McReynolds wrote the opinion. Justice McReynolds wrote that by its very nature, the traditional American understanding of the term liberty prevented the state from forcing students to accept instruction only from public schools.

**Coronation Oath Act 1688-** Prohibits Catholics and their spouses from the Throne of England. ***This act is part of British law to this day!***

-When a priest is ordained, his hands are anointed with oil. Afterwards, he cleans them with a linen cloth called a maniturgium. The priest keeps the maniturgium, and at his mother's funeral, will place it in her hands to be buried with her. The custom is that when she appears at

---

[66]

http://www.kofc.org/rc/en/about/activities/community/pledgeAllegiance.pdf

the pearly gates, she carries this cloth as a sign that she gave God a priest!

**Devil's Door-** Older churches had a small door in the north wall or baptistery called a Devil's Door. The door was left open a crack during a Baptism so the devil could escape.

**-In 2003, over 100,000 Catholics went to prison because of their faith.**[67]

## Catholic Clothes

The following are from the website of St. Ignatius Loyola Catholic Church in Ontario, Canada (footnoted).

**"A Clothes Call ...** Clothing was probably the last thing the Apostles and early Christians had on their minds in the years following the crucifixion. Because they believed the second coming of Christ was imminent, they didn't bother to formalize many aspects of their new religion. Clerical dress was no exception - nobody gave any thought to what priests should wear during Mass; they just wore the same clothes that laypeople did. As author Adrian Fortescue put it in his book *The Vestments of the Roman Rite*, "Every vestment now worn by a Latin priest, every one worn by a Latin bishop (except the mitre), represents an article of ordinary Roman dress, such as was worn by Christians

---

[67] http://www.theflorentine.net/articles/article-view.asp?issuetocID=1422

all over the Roman Empire in the second, third and fourth centuries."'[68]

Fashions changed over time, but the priests didn't. They stuck with the same clothes they had always worn ... until their garments became so different from what everyone else was wearing that they were associated exclusively with religious life. Some examples:

**The MITRE-** **"Description:** The pointed hat that popes and bishops wear. The *Catholic Encyclopedia* describes it as "a folding hat, made up of two equal, cone-shaped parts that rise to a divided peak at the top." It gets its name from *mitra*, the Greek word for "turban."

**Origin:** Why does the pope wear a pointy hat? To keep his head warm - at least that's what it was for in the old days. Much like today, the popes of antiquity were elderly men who needed protection from the cold. So they wore simple cone-shaped hats, "the headgear of respectable men of the period," when they went outdoors. The hats didn't become purely ceremonial until much later.

**Historical Note:** The mitre started out as a short pointed cap, but by the twelfth century it had grown much taller and evolved from the closed cone shape into the open, two-pointed (one in front and back like they do now. That created a problem. The points reminded people so much of the devil that they became

---

[68] http://www.st-ignatius-loyola.com/triva_pointy-hat.html

known as horns ... so the popes rotated their hats ninety degrees. They've worn them that way ever since."[69]

**The Alb- "Description:** The floor-length white robe the priest wears over his street clothing during Mass.

**Origin:** The alb is a direct descendant of the Roman *tunic*, a shirt-like garment that reached all the way to the wearer's feet. Its name comes from *tunica alba*, which means "white tunic" in Latin."[70]

**The Cincture- "Description:** The ropelike belt the priest uses to tie the alb around his waist.

**Origin:** Loose tunics were the mark of uncouth foreigners in the Roman Empire, where it was considered "slovenly, effeminate, and disrespectful" to wear a garment that wasn't gathered at the waist. People used just about anything as belts ... even ropes."[71]

**The Stole- "Description:** The scarf-like vestment the priest wears over the alb.

**Origin:** Magistrates and public officials of the Roman Empire wore stoles as a symbol of their authority. Priests wore them, too, after the empire converted to Christianity."[72]

**The Chasuble- "Description:** The large outer garment the priest wears at Mass.

---

[69] http://www.st-ignatius-loyola.com/triva_pointy-hat.html
[70] Ibid.
[71] Ibid.
[72] Ibid.

**Origin:** The chasuble was the raincoat of the Greco-Roman world. Today's version is shaped like a poncho - it's almost long enough to touch the floor in front and back but is short enough on the sides for the priest to stick his hands out. The original version was much more cumbersome: It was long all the way around, kind of like a skirt you wore around your neck, and had a hood. It got its name from *casula*, the Latin word for "little house," and was so bulky that a deacon had to stand behind the priest during Mass and gather the garment so that it wouldn't fall over his hands."[73]

**The Roman Collar- "Description:** The stiff Roman collar is the standard street shirt for priests. Only the white part is called the collar; the black part is called a "rabat."

**Origin:** "Originally," says the Reverend Henry McCloud in his book *Clerical Dress and Insignia of the Roman Catholic Church*, the Roman collar "was nothing else than the shirt collar turned down over the cleric's everyday common dress in compliance with a fashion that began toward the end of the sixteenth century. For when the laity began to turn down their collars, the clergy also took up the mode."

... But that's only half the story. The clergy also adopted the fad of lining their collars with fancy lace and needlework, which made them more beautiful but also more difficult to clean. So a third custom arose: covering the collar with a changeable sleeve of white linen to protect it from dirt. The modest-minded Pope

---

[73] http://www.st-ignatius-loyola.com/triva_pointy-hat.html

Urban VIII banned the use of lace in 1624 ... but he didn't ban the protective sleeve. "Thus," McCloud says, "the narrow band of white linen used to protect the collar in the course of a few centuries became what is known today as the Roman collar.""[74]

-The standard **cassock** has 33 buttons, to signify the age of Christ at his crucifixion.

---

[74] http://www.st-ignatius-loyola.com/triva_pointy-hat.html

# Chapter Fourteen
# Recipes

I promised you recipes, didn't I? Thanks so much to my friends for sharing their favorite recipes, and I hope you enjoy them.

## Meat Dishes

### Deer (or beef) Jerky-Oven Method
Rodney Credeur

Slice meat thin, 1/8-1/4 inch. Cut into jerky-sized pieces, about ¾ inch by 3-4 inches long. Lay meat out on a large pan, and season with:
-onion powder
-garlic powder
-red pepper
-white pepper
-black pepper
-DO NOT USE SALT, the Soy Sauce has plenty.

Mix meat around pan so seasoning coats both sides. Repeat until all meat is seasoned.
In a separate bowl, add Soy sauce, a couple of teaspoons of liquid smoke and two heaping tablespoons brown sugar. Cover bowl with foil and refrigerate <u>24 hours.</u>

The next day, prepare oven by moving one rack all the way to the bottom and the other rack all the way to the top. Cover bottom rack with foil to catch drips.

Run a wooden toothpick through the end of a piece of meat and hang on top rack. Continue until all meat is hanging.

Make a ball of foil, and close oven door on foil until about a one inch crack remains. Turn oven to warm, <u>not</u> low.

Cook about 2-1/2 hours or until thickest pieces are no longer spongy.

## Chicken & Sausage Sauce Piquant'
Guy Romero

1 Chicken    Cut into pieces and seasoned.
 May substitute 3# boneless skinless breast or thighs.
2# Sausage    Smoked or fresh sausage.
If smoked, cut into 2 inch pieces. If fresh, do not cut until after sausage is browned in oil.
1/2 C Cooking oil.
4 Lg onions cut into 8 sections.
5 Lg green or red bell peppers cut into 8 sections.
4 Ribs celery cut into 2 inch pieces.
Garlic As much as you possibly can stand. Whole or roughly chopped.
2 Tbsp Roux
1/4C Worcestershire Sauce.
4 -15oz Tomato sauce.
4 -10oz Rotel with juice.
1 6 oz Tomato paste.
1C Water.
Stage one:
Brown chicken pieces in oil a few at a time. Remove and set aside. Brown sausage next. Set aside.
Add onions and peppers until hot, not soft. Add roux and stir until dissolved.

Place chicken and sausage back into pot. Add remaining ingredients, cooking on medium heat.
Stir about every 20 minutes. Cook for 1 hour.

Adjust seasoning, cook some rice!

## Easy Oven Chicken Stew
Louise Comeaux

1 Large fryer, cut up, skinned
1 package of dry Lipton onion soup mix.
1 can of cream of mushroom soup
1 can of mushroom gravy (little yellow can)
1 tsp. Kitchen Bouquet
¾ cup water
¼ cup green onions
¼ cup parsley
½ cup chicken broth
Seasoning to taste

Preheat oven to 375. Season fryer in pot. Mix together all other ingredients except for green onions and pour over chicken. Bake covered 1-1/2 hours. Uncover, sprinkle green onions on top and continue to cook uncovered for ½ hour. Serve over rice.

## Squirrel Sauce Piquante
Walter Comeaux Jr.

17 Squirrels (or rabbits), marinated if preferred
3 cans tomato sauce
2 lb. onion, chopped
2 heads garlic
4 stalks celery, chopped
2 bell peppers, chopped
Cooking oil
4 tbsp. flour
Salt and pepper to taste

Cut up meat and season. Add cooking oil to pot and brown meat over medium-high heat. Add small amounts of water from time to time to prevent sticking. Remove meat.
Make a small roux in pot with oil and flour (4 tbsp.). When roux is done, add onions and small amount of water. Cook until tender. Add bell peppers, garlic and celery. Add tomato sauce and extra water if it becomes too thick. Simmer until vegetables are tender. Add meat and simmer until tender. Season to taste, serve over rice.

## Mexican Cornbread
Shirley Boutte

1 can Mexicorn (drained)
2 boxes Jiffy corn muffin mix
3 eggs
2-1/2 cups milk
1 lb. Velveeta chopped very small
1 onion (optional)
1 tsp. salt
3 tsp. sugar
½ cup oil
3-4 tsp. jalapeño-chopped
1 lb. ground meat or breakfast sausage

Brown meat and drain.
Add all ingredients together in a 9X12 pan.
Bake at 350 degrees for 55 minutes.
*I usually use a little less than 1 lb. of cheese. Using an electric knife makes it easier to cut into small pieces. Recipe can be doubled if you have a larger baking pan.

## Pork Steak
Guy Romero

Ask your butcher to cut a Boston Butt Roast into ¾ inch steaks. A Boston Butt roast will make about 10 steaks and cost about a dollar per steak! Watch the Piggly Wiggly sale papers or check with your local butcher. They go on sale quite often.

Preheat your oven to 350, or light the pit.
Using a large pot, heat a bit of oil over medium-high heat.
Season both sides of the steaks with your choice of seasoning.
Brown the steaks on both sides.
Place each steak on a sheet of aluminum foil, and pour your favorite BBQ sauce over it.
Wrap the steak in the aluminum foil and place in the oven or on the pit.
If you cook them in the oven, place a pan under the steaks since the juices may leak.
Bake or BBQ for about one hour.

# Seafood Dishes

### Ed's Fried Fish Tip
The next time you fry fish, try battering the fish in your favorite chicken wing sauce, then bread and fry like you normally do!

### Crawfish Fettuccini
Guy Romero

| | |
|---|---|
| 3# | Peeled Crawfish Tails |
| 1# | Velveeta Jalapeno Cheese |
| 3/4# | Unsalted Butter |
| 1 | Pint Heavy Cream |
| 1 | Large Onion, Chopped |
| 1 | Large Bell Pepper, Chopped |
| 1 | Rib Celery, Chopped |
| 1 | Can Rotel Tomatoes, Drained |
| 1C | Bread Crumbs |
| 1# | Fettuccini |
| 1/2c | Scallions, Chopped |

Sautee onion, pepper, and celery in butter till clear. Add flour, cook for 10 minutes stirring constantly not to burn. Boil pasta in separate pot. Add crawfish and Rotel to vegetables and cook covered 10 minutes. Add cream & cheese, bring to simmer. Drain Pasta, add to crawfish. Stir in scallions. Add your favorite
seasonings to taste. Place into buttered casserole dish, top with bread crumbs. Bake covered 30 minutes at 350 degrees. Remove cover to brown bread crumbs if desired. Serves 8-10.

**Crawfish Cornbread**
Linda Robicheaux

1 pound crawfish
2 cups yellow cornmeal
3 eggs 1 can cream style corn
1 1/2 cups grated cheddar cheese
3/4 cup onion tops 1 jalepeno peppers, finely chopped
1 chopped onion 1/2 cup chopped bell pepper
1/2 tsp baking soda 1 tsp salt
1/2 cup oil 3 tsp baking powder
1 cup milk

Saute onions and bell peppers in a small amount of butter until the
onions are transparent. Add jalepeno peppers and set aside.
Mix together all other ingredients, except crawfish. Add in cooked
onions and peppers. Stir in crawfish.

Pour into a lightly greased 13 x 9 pan and bake at 400 degrees for 35-40 minutes.

**Coconut Shrimp**
Alex Romero

24 Large shrimp peeled and de-veined, seasoned with your favorite seasoning.
2 cups cornstarch.
2 cups coconut flakes.
2 cups panko(Japanese bread crumbs) May substitute cracker crumbs.
6 whipped egg whites.
Vegetable oil for frying heated to 350 degrees.

Dredge seasoned shrimp in cornstarch until coated. Dip into egg whites. Coat with mixture of coconut and panko. Press mixture onto shrimp and set aside for a couple minutes to allow coating mixture to absorb liquid from egg whites. Place shrimp into oil one at a time to prevent sticking to each other. Turn shrimp two or three times while frying to allow even cooking. Do not place too many shrimp into oil at the same time, this will reduce the temperature allowing oil to soak into shrimp. Remove when golden. See dipping sauce below:

Sweet and Sour Dipping Sauce
¾ cup Brown Sugar
½ cup Vinegar
1 tsp Salt
5 Tbsp Ketchup
¾ cup Pineapple Juice
2 Tbsp Cornstarch

Place all ingredients into saucepan except cornstarch. Bring to simmer. Add cornstarch, stirring constantly until thick. Diced onion and peppers of any kind are a great addition to this sauce.

Try dipping hot fresh shrimp right into this sauce when removing from oil, then place shrimp on rack to allow sauce to dry slightly.

## Drunken Crawfish Pie
Guy Romero

| | |
|---|---|
| 2# | Peeled Crawfish Tails |
| ¼# | Unsalted Butter |
| 1 | Medium Onion, Chopped |
| 1 | Lg Bell Pepper, Chopped (Red Preferred) |
| 1 | Rib Celery, Chopped |
| 2tsp | Minced Garlic |
| 1/4C | Flour |
| 1/4C | Scallions, Chopped |
| 1/2C | Heavy Cream |
| 1/4C | Brandy |
| 4 | Pre Prepared Pie Shells or Equivalent |

Sautee vegetables in butter until soft. Add flour, stir 10 minutes as not to burn flour. Add tails and heavy cream, simmer covered 10 minutes. Stir in scallions and brandy. Allow to cool at least 30 minutes. Pour into two pie shells and cover with two pie shells. Vent center of top shell. Bake at 375 degrees 25-30 minutes.

## Shrimp and Tasso Pasta
Louise Comeaux

1 stick of butter
1 Tasso
1 lb. peeled shrimp
1 jar store-bought Alfredo sauce
1 pint heavy cream
1 box bowtie pasta
Freshly grated Parmesan cheese

Cook pasta as per directions. Meanwhile, melt butter in skillet. Add tasso and sauté to render fat.
Add shrimp and cook until pink and curled, taking care not to burn butter.
Add Alfredo sauce and stir to incorporate.
Add heavy cream and bring to a boil. Do not allow the sauce to reduce.
Pour heated pasta into a serving bowl. Pour sauce over pasta.
Top with parmesan cheese.

**Rod's Fried Crab Cakes**
Rodney Credeur

2 bottles clam juice
2 medium Irish potatoes
1 can crab meat
Onion tops
Seasoning
1 egg
Milk
Seasoned bread crumbs

Boil potatoes in clam juice until tender. Mash potatoes and add crab meat. You can also add sac-a-lait, bream or other cooked fish (flaked apart). Mix well
Form into patties, dip in egg and milk wash and coat with seasoned bread crumbs.
Fry to a golden brown.


**Baked like Fried Fish**
Louise Comeaux

Fish fillets
Buttery Ritz Crackers- finely crumbled
Margarine
Seasoning

Lay fillets in a baking pan and season. Place a couple of dabs of margarine on each fillet and season. Sprinkle each fillet with about ¼ inch of crumbled Ritz crackers. Bake at 350 degrees until done. Gives your fillets a great breaded coating without frying!

## Low-Fat Crawfish Fettuccini
Mary Laurent

1 medium onion, chopped
1 medium bellpepper, chopped
1/2 to 3/4 cup chopped celery
1 small can V-8 juice
2 cans fat-free cream of mushroom soup
1 can fat-free cream of celery soup
Lite Velveeta cheese or sliced fat-free cheese to taste
2 lbs. crawfish, rinsed well and cleaned of all fat
red pepper to taste
oregano to taste
parsley to taste
milk to taste
3/4 cup chopped onion tops
boiled fetuccine noodles (or linguine if you prefer)

Boil noodles according to package directions. In a large saucepan or roaster, saute onions, celery and bellpepper in V-8 juice until wilted. Add soups. Stir well and slowly bring to a simmer. Add crawfish and let simmer for about 10-15 minutes. Stir often. Add as much cheese as you like (I usually use about a cup of Velveeta Lite chopped in little blocks to melt faster). Keep simmering until cheese melts. If mixture is too thick for your liking, add fat-free or skim milk until it gets to desired consistency. Stir often and keep simmering. Add at least 1 tablespoon oregano and parsley. Add red pepper to mixture, stir well and taste. Adjust seasonings and add chopped onion tops. Stir well. Mix well with noodles and serve immediately.

**Stuffed Crabs**
Rodney Credeur

1 dozen live crabs
Oil
1 onion
½ bell pepper
4 cloves garlic
4 stalks celery
Dry dressing mix
Parsley
1 tsp. Kitchen Bouquet
Red Pepper
Salt
Bread Crumbs

Boil crabs in seasoned water, about 30 minutes. Cool. Pry open crab shells (saving top shell). Remove all white meat and a little fat and set aside.
Scrub shells in clean water. Drop in boiling water with a pinch of soda about 20 minutes. Allow shells to cool.
Sautee chopped onion, bell pepper, garlic and celery in oil about 5 minutes. Add crabmeat and brown. Add a little crab fat, butter and water to moisten. Add red pepper, salt, Kitchen Bouquet. Cover and simmer 30 minutes or until water is absorbed. Mix with dry dressing and stuff shells. Top with bread crumbs. Bake 20-25 minutes at 350 degrees.

## Shrimp and Pasta Casserole
Mary Laurent

2 pounds peeled and deveined shrimp
3 sticks butter
1 onion, chopped
1 bellpepper, chopped
1 stalk celery, chopped
1 lb. Mexican Velveeta
1 pint whipping Cream
16 oz. Wide Egg Noodles, cooked according to directions
½ cup parsley flakes
Seasoning to taste

Saute' onions, bellpepper and celery in butter. In a dutch oven, combine vegetables, whipping cream, velveeta, parsley and shrimp, and cook on a low-medium heat until cheese is melted and shrimp are cooked. Mix with cooked pasta and serve or pour into a greased 9 x 13 casserole dish for reheating later. Cover and bake at 350 degrees until heated through.

## Crawfish Potato Soup
Guy Romero

5#     Russet potatoes. Peeled and diced into ½" cubes.
1#     Bacon. Sliced into ½" strips.
2      Lg onions finely chopped.
2      Lg bell pepperd diced.
1C     shredded or finely chopped carrots.
2#     Corn. Any kind will do. Roasted is best
1      Pint heavy cream
1      Quart whole milk.
2Tbsp  Crab boil seasoning.
1#     Peeled crawfish tails.
1      Bunch scallions chopped coarsely.

Boil potatoes until fork tender in just enough water to cover potatoes. Do not drain. In second pot, render bacon until cooked. Add onions, peppers, carrots and corn. Cook until soft, then add to potatoes. Add milk and cream simmering on low fire about 20 minutes. Add remaining ingredients and simmer about 10 minutes. Do not over cook crawfish.
Serve with toasted French bread.

## Corn and Crab Bisque
David Laurent

1 medium onion, finely chopped
1 stick butter
1 box 10-12 oz. Frozen corn
2 Tablespoons flour
1 16 oz. Bottle clam juice
1 lb. Crabmeat
1 16 oz. Carton half and half

Saute' onion in butter until wilted. Chop ½ cup frozen corn in food processor or blender. Add corn to onion and butter mixture. Cook for four minutes. Season with salt and white pepper. Add flour, clam juice and half and half. Heat until hot. Add crabmeat. Heat for a few more minutes and serve. Serve with 2 drops of Tabasco and a sprig of parsley on top.
Serving suggestions:
This recipe doubles easily and can be made with crawfish or shrimp if crabmeat is not in season. Be sure to coarsely chop the <u>well-rinsed</u> crawfish or shrimp before adding to the soup. It also freezes beautifully.

This soup is really delicious and is excellent served in bread bowls you purchase at your local bakery (Poupart's in Lafayette has great bread bowls). Slice off just the top of the bread bowl, dig out the inside of the bread bowl, being careful not to take out too much and puncture the sides of the bowls. Toast in a warm oven before serving. Place the top of the bowl back on after ladling in the soup to keep it nice and hot or use them for dipping. After eating a bowl or two of the soup, eat the bowl too!

## Shrimp and Pesto Salad
Mary Laurent

2 pounds shrimp, peeled and deveined
1 Jar pesto (7oz.)
1 red onion chopped
½ bottle Girard's Caesar dressing
½ bottle Girard's Champagne dressing
1 16 oz. Package Bowtie pasta, cooked according to directions
Romaine Lettuce, torn into small pieces
Grated parmesan cheese

Sauté' shrimp in pesto. Let chill. Boil pasta according to directions and let chill. Both of these steps can be done the day before. When ready to serve, combine the shrimp/pesto combination with the onions, the salad dressings and the cheese. Mix well then toss with the pasta and lettuce just before serving so the lettuce won't wilt.

# Side Dishes

### Sweet Potato Souffle'
Guy Romero

| | |
|---|---|
| 2# | Peeled Sweet Potatos |
| 3/4C | Brown Sugar |
| 3/4C | Granulated Sugar |
| 2TBSP | Flour |
| 1 1/2tsp | Baking Powder |
| 1 1/2tsp | Vanilla Extract |
| 3 | Large Eggs, room temperature |
| 1/4C | Soft Unsalted Butter |

Boil potatos till fork tender, drain, and set aside. Preheat oven to 350 degrees. Puree Potatoes with sugars. Add flour, baking powder, vanilla and blend. Add eggs, blending between each. Butter baking dish and coat with brown sugar. Pour mixture into dish. Bake 45 minutes testing for doneness when center is firm to the touch turn off oven, opend door to allow soufflé to cool 10 minutes before removing. See topping below.

Caramelized Pecan Topping
3/4C   Butter
3/4C   Chopped Pecans
1/2C   Brown Sugar

Blend and simmer 10 minutes or until sticky. Pour over soufflé.
Alternate topping of powdered sugar can be used.

## Cheese Olives
Mary Laurent

12 ounces sharp cheddar cheese, grated
2 cups flour
2 sticks butter or margarine, melted
2 large jars stuffed olives (less if you like a lot of batter around your olives)
1 tsp. red pepper
1/4 tsp. salt

Combine flour, salt and red pepper and mix well. Add butter and cheese and mix or knead well. Drain olives. Take a small amount of flour mixture and flatten in your hand. Put an olive on the flour mixture and roll into a ball. Either freeze or bake at 350° for 10-15 minutes. Do not grease pan before baking. These are delicious even if you don't like olives.

## Corn Dip
Mary Laurent

2 green onions chopped
1 cup mayonnaise
10 oz. shredded cheese
2 jalapenos, chopped
2 cans Mexican corn, drained
1 cup sour cream
1 small can green chilies

Combine all ingredients. Serve with chips or best with bagel chips. It's best to make the day ahead you serve it.

## Baked Macaroni
Mary Laurent

1 pk. #7 Macaroni
1pk. mild cheddar cheese (sometime I use a little more)
1 large can of pet milk
3 eggs
3/4 stick of butter or margarine

Boil macaroni, drain, let cool just a little, so that when you add the eggs they won't cook. Beat eggs and pour over the cooked macaroni. Mix well. Butter your 9X12 baking dish real well and pour 1/2 of the macaroni into baking dish. Pour 1/2 of the pet milk and top with 1/2 sliced thin cheese on top of that. Repeat the next layer like the first.

Bale at 350 oven for 1 hour, cover with tin foil that is raised so as not to touch the cheese on top before baking. Bake with the foil on the whole time.

## Big Dave's Salsa
David Laurent

4   100 ounce cans crushed tomatoes
4   100 ounce cans whole peeled tomatoes
3   64 ounce jars sliced jalapeno peppers
1   cup dried cilantro
½   gallon vinegar
50  pounds onions, peeled and quartered
1   box table salt

Heat mixture until boiling. This recipe will make approximately 12 gallons, enough to fill eight (8) dozen pint jars or four (4) dozen quart jars. Pour into sterilized jars and seal.

## Farfalle with Asparagus and Cherry Tomatoes
Mary Laurent

4 tbsp. Olive Oil
¼ cup minced shallots
2 garlic cloves, crushed
¼ cup basil, finely chopped
¼ to ½ cup of lemon juice
¼ cup chopped pecans
¼ cup real bacon bits
1 pound fresh asparagus spears, chopped into 1 ½ inch pieces
1 pint cherry tomatoes, halved or quartered
1 pound farfalle (bow-tie) pasta
Tony Chachere's to taste
¼ cup freshly grated parmesan cheese

Boil pasta according to directions, adding seasoning to the water. About one to two minutes before draining, add asparagus pieces and return to a boil for a minute or two until the asparagus turns bright green and are tender. Drain and rinse with cold water to prevent the asparagus from overcooking.

While pasta is boiling, sauté shallots, bacon and garlic in 3 tbsp. olive oil in a skillet. Add chopped pecans. Continue cooking for one to two minutes. Turn off heat and add ¼ cup lemon juice and stir or whisk.

In a large mixing bowl, mix tomato halves with the basil, 1 tsp. olive oil and ¼ cup lemon juice. Add seasoning to taste.

Once pasta is drained and rinsed, combine everything with the tomato mixture and gently toss, adding the parmesan cheese before tossing. Adjust seasonings to your taste and serve. This is a great cold side dish to serve with burgers or other grilled meats.

**Shrimp Dip**
Mary Laurent
1/2 pint sour cream
1-8 ounce package cream cheese, room temperature
1/2 cup celery, chopped fine
1/2 cup green onions, chopped fine
2 tablespoons mayonnaise
Salt and pepper to taste
3 tablespoons lemon juice
Red pepper to taste
2 small cans shrimp or boiled, chopped and mashed fresh shrimp

Combine sour cream with cream cheese. Add mayonnaise, celery, green onions, salt, pepper, lemon juice and red pepper to taste. Mash the shrimp with a fork or chop in food processor and add to the cheese mixture. Sprinkle red pepper on top and serve. This recipe will make approximately 1 quart and tastes best if prepared a day ahead of serving.

# Desserts

## German Chocolate Crater Cake
Guy Romero

1 cup chopped pecans
1 cup coconut flakes
1 packaged German chocolate cake mix
8 oz cream cheese
1 stick butter(4 oz)
1lb powdered sugar
1 Milky Way candy bar about 2 oz
¾ cup evaporated milk

Preheat oven to 350 degrees. Spray 9" x 13" baking pan with non stick spray. Sprinkle pecans and coconut into baking pan. Melt over low heat, cream cheese and butter, stir in powdered sugar until blended, set aside. Prepare cake mix according to box instructions and pour over coconut and pecans. Spoon cream cheese mixture over cake mix, a piping bag or zip top bag works best for this. Bake cake 40 -45 minutes until done.

While cake is baking, melt milky way and evaporated milk over low heat. Allow cake to cool about 10 -15 minutes. Poke holes in top of cake with fork. Pour Milky Way mixture over cake.

## Millionaire Candy
Rodney Credeur

1 cup sugar
1 cup brown sugar
1 cup white Karo syrup
1 cup margarine (2 sticks)
1 lg. can evaporated milk
4 cups chopped pecans or peanuts
1 tsp. vanilla
1 bag milk chocolate chips

Mix sugars, syrup and margarine with 1 cup evaporated milk and bring to a boil.
Add the rest of the milk and bring to a soft boil stage or 230 degrees.
Add nuts and vanilla.
Pour into pan & cool.
Cut into 1 inch pieces or bars.
Melt chocolate and dip candy to cover.

## Grandi Girl Cake
Guy Romero

2 cups sugar
3 eggs
1 ½ cups vegetable oil
¼ cup orange juice
3 cups all purpose flour
1 tsp. baking soda
¼ tsp. salt
1 tbsp. ground cinnamon
1 tbsp. vanilla extract
3 cups peeled diced apples. Green is best, any will do.
1 cup coconut flakes
1 cup chopped pecans
1 cup dried cranberries

Topping sauce:
1 stick butter
1 cup sugar
½ cup buttermilk
½ tsp. baking soda

Preheat oven to 325 degrees. In a large mixing bowl combine the first 9 ingredients and mix well. Fold in apples, coconuts, pecans and cranberries. Pour batter into greased tube pan and bake 75-90 minutes until toothpick comes out clean. To prepare sauce, place all ingredients into sauce pan, bring to a boil stirring constantly. Boil about 2 minutes. Pour this mixture over cake as soon as the cake is removed from the oven. Let cool a minimum of 1 hour before cutting.

## Bread Pudding
Tina Belaire

7 Regular sized (seedless) hamburger buns
5 eggs
2 cups sugar
2 cups milk
2 teaspoons vanilla
1 large can of crushed pineapples
1 tbsp. butter and ½ cup brown sugar, mixed together for later use

Drain pineapples, beat eggs and white sugar together.
Add vanilla and milk, mix well.
Stir in ¾ can of pineapples then fold in torn hamburger buns. Pour mixture into buttered 8X11 or 8X8 baking dish.
Top with remaining pineapples over pudding.
Apply butter and brown sugar mixture over pudding.
Bake at 350 for 1 hour or until toothpick comes out clean.

Alternate recipe:

Omit pineapples
Add ½ bag of chocolate chips and 8 oz. of chopped pecans to butter and brown sugar mixture and sprinkle on top of pudding before baking. Bake as above.

Made in the USA
Charleston, SC
25 March 2011